Developing a Data Warehouse for the Healthcare Enterprise

Lessons from the Trenches

Third Edition

Developing a Data Warehouse for the Healthcare Enterprise

Lessons from the Trenches

Third Edition

Bryan Bergeron, MD, Editor

Hamad Al-Daig, MBA

Osama Alswailem, MD, MA

Enam UL Hoque, MBA, PMP, CPHIMS

Fadwa Saad AlBawardi, MS

CRC Press

Taylor & Francis Group

Boca Raton London New York

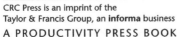

CRC Press is an imprint of the
Taylor & Francis Group, an **informa** business

A PRODUCTIVITY PRESS BOOK

Taylor & Francis
Boca Raton   London   New York
A CRC Press title, part of the Taylor & Francis imprint, a member of the Taylor & Francis Group, the academic division of T&F Informa plc

Published in 2018 by CRC Press
a Taylor & Francis Group
6000 Broken Sound Parkway NW, Suite 300
Boca Raton, FL 33487-2742

Printed in the United States of America on acid-free paper 10 9 8 7 6 5 4 3 2 1

International Standard Book Number-13: 978-1-138-50296-3 (Hardback)
International Standard Book Number-13: 978-1-138-50295-6 (Paperback)
International Standard Book Number-13: 978-1-315-14517-4 (eBook)

Library of Congress Cataloging-in-Publication Data

Names: Bergeron, Bryan P., author. | Alswailem, Osama, author. | Al-Daig,
Hamad, author. | Hoque, Enam UL, author. | AlBawardi, Fadwa Saad, author.
Title: Developing a data warehouse for the healthcare enterprise : lessons
from the trenches / Bryan Bergeron, Osama Alswailem, Hamad Al-Daig, Enam
UL Hoque, Fadwa Saad AlBawardi.
Description: Third edition. | Boca Raton : Taylor & Francis, 2018. | Includes
bibliographical references and index.
Identifiers: LCCN 2017056424| ISBN 9781138502963 (hardback : alk. paper) |
ISBN 9781138502956 (paperback : alk. paper) | ISBN 9781315145174 (ebook)
Subjects: LCSH: Medical care--Information technology. | Medical care--Data
processing.
Classification: LCC R858 .B4714 2018 | DDC 610.285--dc23
LC record available at https://lccn.loc.gov/2017056424

Visit the Taylor & Francis Web site at
http://www.taylorandfrancis.com

and the CRC Press Web site at
http://www.crcpress.com

HIMSS Mission

To lead healthcare transformation through the effective use of health information technology.

Printed in the U.S.A. 5 4 3 2 1

Requests for permission to make copies of any part of this work should be sent to:
Permissions Editor
HIMSS
33 W. Monroe St., #1700
Chicago, IL 60603-5616
nvitucci@himss.org

The inclusion of an organization name, product, or service in this publication should not be considered as an endorsement of such organization, product, or service, nor is the failure to include an organization name, product, or service to be construed as disapproval.

For more information about HIMSS, please visit www.himss.org.

Contents

Preface

This is the third edition of *Developing a Data Warehouse for the Healthcare Enterprise: Lessons from the Trenches*, the first edition having received the 2008 HIMSS Book of the Year Award. The primary goal of this book is to provide an up-to-date, straightforward view of a clinical data warehouse project at King Faisal Specialist Hospital and Research Centre (KFSH&RC) in Riyadh, Saudi Arabia. Whereas the first two editions emphasized inception and implementation, this third edition looks at the mature project with an eye toward the maintenance phase of the life cycle.

Despite an uptick in data warehouse implementations in the healthcare sector over the past decade, the definitions of exactly what constitutes a data warehouse still vary from one vendor and healthcare enterprise to the next. For the purpose of this book, a data warehouse is defined as a logically central repository for selected clinical and nonclinical data from disparate, often loosely integrated systems throughout the healthcare enterprise. In our case, the logically central repository is also physically central.

From a strategic perspective, the data warehouse is an enabling technology that, when properly implemented, can be leveraged to reduce medical errors, promote patient safety, support the development of an enterprise-wide electronic health record (EHR), and support process/work flow redesign. As such, the upside potential for a successful data warehouse implementation is enormous. However, as with any large-scale, expensive, mission-critical IT project, an inferior implementation can spell disaster for not only the IT department staff but for the healthcare enterprise as a whole.

The venue for our discussion, KFSH&RC, is a large, modern, tertiary-care hospital in Saudi Arabia with an environment that parallels leading-edge U.S. hospitals. The clinical departments, surgical wards, operating rooms, bedside monitors, and even the formularies are indistinguishable from those in a tertiary-care hospital in Boston, New York, or San Francisco. There is even a Starbucks in the main lobby, albeit with palm trees and camels on the souvenir coffee mugs.

More importantly, the IT environment is indistinguishable from the best in the United States, with hardware from the likes of IBM and HP, and an EHR system from Cerner. Given this infrastructure, which includes a data warehouse, it's no surprise that KFSH&RC is the first HIMSS Analytics Stage 7–certified hospital in the Middle East. Moreover, KFSH&RC is leveraging the data warehouse in a proteomics initiative that has brought the enterprise to the forefront of translational medicine.

In addition to reviewing the experiences at KFSH&RC, we examine the value of the data warehouse from the U.S. perspective. We discuss the increasing role of data analytics in supporting an era of increased accountability and personal expense for care in the United States. As a result, the lessons learned should have both domestic and international appeal and applicability.

This book is written for the HIMSS membership—including chief information officers (CIOs), IT managers, and hospital administrators—involved in medical error reduction, patient safety, EHR implementation, and process improvement. It is designed as a road map for healthcare enterprise executives and IT managers contemplating or already involved in a data warehouse implementation. Although the contributors are obviously biased proponents of data warehouse technology, they are quick to point out some of the difficulties and limitations faced during the implementation process and ways to either avoid or overcome them.

The chapters, written by those responsible for different aspects of the project, tell all from personal, hands-on experience. The original contributors have updated their respective chapters to reflect changes since the second edition. The timely update makes this book a must-have for owners of the first and second editions, as well as new readers.

This book is unique in that it provides the perspectives of several key stakeholders in the data warehouse development project at KFSH&RC, from the initial vision to release. We provide the view of the CIO (Hamad Al-Daig), the medical informatician (Osama Alswailem), the technical manager (Enam UL Hoque), the senior program analyst (Fadwa AlBawardi), and the external consultant (Bryan Bergeron). The internal parallels and occasional contradictions exemplify the challenges readers should consider in their own data warehouse development projects. As such, this book also provides insight into the inner workings of a large healthcare enterprise—in itself a valuable resource for healthcare IT professionals.

Developing a Data Warehouse for the Healthcare Enterprise is structured as stand-alone chapters written from different perspectives. Readers are forewarned that, unlike some edited collections that strive for a single voice and perspective, there are numerous points of view that are, on occasion, in apparent contradiction in approach or ranking of importance. These differences in perspective are celebrated and emphasized to illustrate the real-world differences in how a CIO approaches an implementation challenge compared with, for example, a consultant or information systems architect.

Chapter 1, "Here, There Be Monsters," explores the risks and potential upsides of embarking on a data warehouse initiative. It serves as both a sanity check and a gut check for those contemplating the move.

Chapter 2, "The Data Warehouse as Feeder to Data Analytics and Business Intelligence: The Good, the Great, the Bad and the Ugly," explores the relationship of data analytics and business intelligence to decision support and compares decision support based on a data warehouse versus disparate sources.

Chapter 3, "Enterprise Environment," provides an overview of our enterprise environment from an operational prospective, including clinical load, IT infrastructure, and organizational structure.

Chapter 4, "Vendor Selection and Management," provides an overview of request for proposal (RFP) development, vendor selection, and the management processes that were integral to the development of the data warehouse.

Chapter 5, "Development Team," provides an overview of the human resources involved in the data warehouse project, from team formulation to the assignment of roles and responsibilities.

Chapter 6, "Planning," provides an overview of the preparation that went into data warehouse implementation.

Chapter 7, "Design," provides an overview of our technical design, including the data model, logical, and physical architecture; the extraction, transformation, and loading (ETL) process; provision for backup and recovery; and reporting.

Chapter 8, "KPI Selection," explores the process used to determine the most appropriate key performance indicators (KPIs) for our data warehouse implementation.

Chapter 9, "Implementation," describes the highlights of our implementation process, including the ETL build, the online analytical processing (OLAP) build, and user acceptance testing.

Chapter 10, "Post-implementation Organizational Structure," describes the plans defined by management to address the issues of ownership, roles, and responsibilities associated with the data warehouse.

Chapter 11, "Report Life Cycle," defines the data warehouse–based reporting system life cycle, from generation to retirement.

Chapter 12, "Knowledge Transfer," details our approach to managing the transfer of intellectual assets associated with the development of our data warehouse from vendors and consultants to our permanent staff.

The epilogue provides a compilation of the lessons learned from the preceding chapters and discusses their applicability to other data warehouse projects.

Because a data warehouse is a compilation of applications and technologies, numerous acronyms are inevitable. As such, the section entitled "Acronyms" defines the major ones readers are likely to encounter in a data warehouse initiative. Similarly, one of the greatest hurdles for IT executives working with leading-edge technologies in a healthcare organization is using the appropriate terminology when communicating with vendors, engineers, and administrators. The glossary is intended to help bridge the vocabulary gap.

Bryan Bergeron, MD
Boston, Massachusetts

Acknowledgments

Sharing the lessons learned—the hard way—of a major healthcare IT project is no mean feat, even with time for reflection and the benefit of 20/20 hindsight. Actually facing the day-to-day challenges of implementing a multimillion dollar project tests the mettle of even the most seasoned healthcare CIO and management team. Then there are the myriad challenges associated with maintenance, where considerable resources can be spent simply to keep the system functioning even though the world may be in political and economic chaos.

The contributors to this book deserve special acknowledgment for sharing their boots-on-the-ground experiences without the sugar-coating that authors often use for self-promotion. You'll read accounts of what actually transpired during the development of data warehouses—the good, the great, the bad, and the ugly—and take away pearls of wisdom on what to emulate and what to avoid. We believe that knowing what to avoid, and what doesn't work, is at least as important as being able to differentiate what *can* be done from what *should* be done. Learning from the successes and failures of others is more fruitful and less costly than stumbling across your successes and learning from your own mistakes. Moreover, the benefits of such learning accrue to both the individual and the healthcare institution.

Thanks also to those who have been instrumental in the ongoing development of the data warehouse at KFSH&RC, especially Wadood Tafiq, director, Data and Analytics.

About the Editor

Bryan Bergeron, MD, a fellow of the American College of Medical Informatics, is the author of numerous books, articles, software packages, and patents. He has practiced medical informatics at Massachusetts General Hospital in Boston and taught medical informatics, as well as traditional medical courses, in the Health Sciences and Technology division of Harvard Medical School and MIT for nearly three decades. He has been involved in the development of the data warehouse at King Faisal Specialist Hospital and Research Centre (KFSH&RC) since the inception of the project.

About the Authors

Hamad Al-Daig, MBA, is a retired chief information officer (CIO) at King Faisal Specialist Hospital and Research Centre (KFSH&RC). He has over 35 years of healthcare IT experience, 28 of those years with KFSH&RC. During his tenure, the hospital attained EMR Adoption Level 6 and ISO 27001 Information Security Management certification. As a leading distinguished professional in healthcare IT, he has contributed to many national-level healthcare IT initiatives, including the development of the national healthcare IT strategy for Saudi Arabia. He is the co-founder and vice president of the Saudi Arabian Health Informatics (SAHI) society. He has been named one of the top 10 CIO innovators of the year by Healthcare Informatics. He is as an emeritus member in good status with KLAS, having served as an international advisory board member for the company. Hamad is CEO of Carelink, a healthcare IT company in Saudi Arabia.

Osama Alswailem, MD, MA, a consultant in family medicine and CIO of KFSH&RC, is the former director of the Medical and Clinical Informatics department. Dr. Alswailem received his medical degree and his board certification in family and community medicine from the College of Medicine, King Saud University, Saudi Arabia. He also obtained a master's degree while completing a postdoctoral fellowship in medical informatics at Columbia University, New York. In addition to his hospital duties, Dr. Alswailem is an assistant professor at Alfaisal University, where he teaches medical informatics.

Enam UL Hoque, MBA, PMP, CPHIMS, is a senior strategic health information consultant at KFSH&RC. He is currently playing an advisory role to the CIO and other C-Suite members within the hospital. Previously, he managed the technical areas of the initial data warehouse development project and introduced performance improvement through the Productivity Analysis and Benchmarking program for the hospital. He is an IT professional with more than 25 years of experience, holding various positions and managing IT projects of varying sizes within industries ranging from manufacturing and retail to marketing and healthcare in Canada, the United States, and Saudi Arabia.

Fadwa Saad AlBawardi, MS, is the Acting Director, Business and Intelligence Management, ISID, Ministry of National Guard Health Affairs, Riyadh. Ms. AlBawardi formerly worked as a project leader and senior program analyst for the data warehouse section, Healthcare Information Technology Affairs at KFSH&RC in Riyadh. Ms AlBawardi received her MS in computer science at Boston University, Massachusetts, and has been working in the data warehousing/business intelligence areas for several years.

Chapter 1

Here, There Be Monsters

Bryan Bergeron

Contents

Introduction

In medieval Europe, the ocean was the great unknown, fraught with dangers as well as the promise of riches. The life of a captain was a perilous one, in that death could come at any time from bad weather or, even worse, attack by one of the many monsters that supposedly inhabited the ocean. As I've depicted in Figure 1.1, maps of the time often had explicit indications of the dangers lurking in the ocean. Of course, as the centuries passed and new technologies were developed, we came to know the earth as a sphere spinning in space instead of a flat surface, and the sea monsters were either disproven or became sources of food and fuel, fodder for academic studies, and, finally, endangered species on the edge of extinction.

Today, the chief information officer (CIO) of a hospital or healthcare enterprise is a high-risk profession. Based on my ad hoc research, I'd say

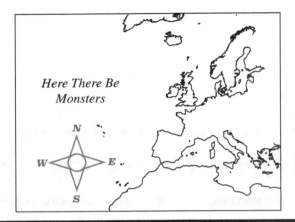

Figure 1.1   Common perception of the ocean as depicted on medieval maps.

that two years is the average tenure of a healthcare CIO. This relatively high turnover is due in part to the CIO's inability to deliver on time and on budget, given the ever-changing political, regulatory, and economic foundations of healthcare and the resulting changes in IT projects. There are just too many unknowns—potential monsters out there, if you will— at the time of planning. And when the monsters do appear, it's often too late to change course. Given this reality, why would a healthcare CIO add a data warehouse implementation—recognized as an extremely high-risk proposition[1,2]—to their list of promises? As with the seafaring captains of old, we take the risk because of the promise of significant rewards.

So, what sort of rewards are we talking about? Well, consider that by integrating disparate clinical and administrative data sources into a single source model, a data warehouse can provide clinicians, administrators, and researchers with information from a variety of otherwise noncompatible or poorly integrated sources. Moreover, the data can be had in seconds to minutes, when it has value in clinical decision making, as opposed to days or weeks later. A properly constructed and maintained data warehouse supports *rapid* data mining, *rapid* report generation, and *real-time* decision support—all key components of a full-featured electronic health record (EHR) or electronic medical record (EMR).

Another reward to consider in the risk/reward calculation is recognition by your peers and your institution. Easily at the top of my list for bragging rights is attaining Stage 7 certification of the HIMSS Analytics EMR Adoption Model. As shown in Table 1.1, a data warehouse is one of the four prerequisites for Stage 7 certification. However, there remains the

Table 1.1 Eight Stages of the HIMSS Analytics EMR Adoption Model, with the data warehouse in Stage 7

Stage	Cumulative Capabilities
7	Data warehouse Complete EHR CCD (cash concentration and disbursement) transactions to share data Data continuity with emergency department, ambulatory, and outpatient
6	Physician documentation (structured templates) Full clinical decision support system (variance and compliance) Full radiology picture archiving communications system
5	Closed loop medication administration
4	Computerized physician order entry CDS (clinical protocols)
3	Nursing/clinical documentation (flow sheets) CDS system (error checking) PACS available outside radiology
2	Clinical data repository Controlled medical vocabulary CDS May have document imaging Health information exchange capable
1	Lab, radiology, and pharmacy installed
0	No ancillaries installed

economic reality that comes with developing or acquiring a data warehouse; it demands significant human and computer resources over a sustained period of time.

Figure 1.2 provides another view of the data warehouse, in the context of the traditional evolution of healthcare IT capabilities. As shown in the figure, capabilities generally evolve from claims processing to transaction processing to transaction databases, such as those with a particular clinical system. A population of transaction databases—from clinical, administrative, and financial systems—is necessary to feed a comprehensive data warehouse.

As shown in Figure 1.2, there is also an evolutionary path from financial to administrative to clinical computing, culminating in clinical decision support (CDS) capabilities. The latest area of focus at KFSH&RC is IT support

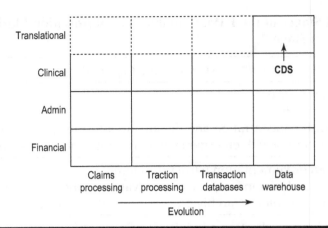

Figure 1.2   Data warehouse in the context of the traditional evolution of healthcare IT capabilities, culminating in CDS capabilities.

for translational medicine, which leverages proteomic data with clinical data residing in the data warehouse.

It's possible to start from scorched earth and purchase an all-in-one EHR solution, complete with a full suite of financial, administrative, and clinical applications, together with a data warehouse, but that's rare. Similarly, it's theoretically possible to skip the financial and administrative processing and go directly to CDS, but such a move is practically impossible. If your institution can't get the bills out, code clinical activities for the maximum legal reimbursement possible, and fulfill administrative obligations, then it won't be operating for long.

For many in the healthcare informatics community, the future of modern medicine is CDS that incorporates both clinical and translational medicine information. For example, when determining whether a patient with a specific genetic predisposition and positive clinical findings should undergo surgical or chemical treatment, the data warehouse serves as an integration enabler for clinical and research computing.

Despite the uncertainties and costs, many in the healthcare industry view adoption of the data warehouse in some form as inevitable once a clear return on investment (ROI) can be identified. In this context, ROI reflects more timely, accurate clinical and administrative data that can form the basis of decisions resulting in cost savings and increased quality of care. These improvements in turn support the goals of *meaningful use*—and are linked to federal incentive funding—as somewhat poorly defined by the HITECH component of the American Recovery and Reinvestment Act of 2009.

One way to address risk, uncertainty, and potential ROI is for organizations involved in data warehouse implementations to share their experiences—whether successful or blatant failures. This chapter provides a general framework for the detailed discussions of the KFSH&RC data warehouse implementation discussed in the following chapters.

Nirvana

To early sailors, mermaids were half-fish, half-women that could lure boats onto the rocks and certain peril. In reality, of course, mermaids were nothing more than manatees. Similarly, to the uninitiated IT professional, the term *data warehouse* often conjures up a vision of a large hard-drive array that holds files from various hospital applications. In reality, a data warehouse is much more. For example, it is comprised of myriad technologies and processes that address three issues in the healthcare enterprise: transparency, standards, and adaptability/performance. To appreciate the significance of these issues, consider the ideal case.

In the future, healthcare CIOs will be able to select from a variety of shrink-wrapped hospital information systems (HISs). Unlike contemporary, disparate HISs, those in the future will run on the same hardware of choice; use a single clinical, administrative, and financial vocabulary; and support the real-time, graphical, and textual reporting of a virtually unlimited number of performance or quality indicators—all without degrading transaction performance. Systems will automatically compile statistics to demonstrate compliance with meaningful-use guidelines and seamlessly integrate with regional and national genomics and proteomics research centers.

Similarly, consider what will happen in this future scenario when the CIO receives a request for a new application—say, a new patient-tracking application based on implantable radio frequency identification (RFID) chips. After some financial and administrative maneuvering, the CIO will give the go-ahead to the development team. A programmer, perhaps offshore, will remotely drag and drop icons from a preconfigured object library. The resulting application will share the same database, vocabulary validation routines, and reporting capabilities as every other application in the system. Creating new printed reports or graphical dashboards will be a cinch, thanks to open, transparent, and documented architecture and database fields.

Despite the introduction of data warehouse appliances, open-source data warehouses, and innovations such as in-memory data warehouses, CIOs and domestic programmers in the healthcare industry need not worry about being replaced by shrink-wrapped HIS application suites any time soon. As of Q3 2016, only 4.5% of hospitals in the United States achieved Stage 7 on the HIMSS Analytics EMR Adoption Model, 30.5 % reached Stage 6, and just over one-third achieved Stage 5.[3] Furthermore, sizeable hospital information systems in the United States typically maintain applications on multiple operating systems and hardware platforms, and IT staff frequently deal with "rogue" departmental applications that require special care and handling, such as support for a legacy operating system or closed database engine.

There are also systemic issues in the healthcare environment beyond the control of the CIO. For example, there is no universal medical identifier in the United States. A seemingly obvious candidate, the Social Security number, is inherently flawed. One of several limitations is that many older women were never issued Social Security cards because it was assumed at one time that women would never work. There are also basic business issues, such as equating proprietary with profit. Consider that no one has been able to convince the likes of Cerner, Epic, GE, or Siemens AG to open up their proprietary databases and system architectures to facilitate integration with third-party applications.

Most hospital information systems are a confederation of variably dependent applications. As such, checking the heartbeat of an information system typically involves multiple queries against multiple systems, often involving mismatched patient identifiers. And then there is the issue of time. Days—and sometimes weeks—are often required to generate and validate complex reports that involve clinical, administrative, and financial data. Such poor performance would not be tolerated on Wall Street or in a typical Fortune 500 company, where time is money. However, it's the norm in healthcare.

As CIO, you have several options to address the transparency, standards, and performance limitations of a typical HIS. Interapplication interfaces, such as HL7, partially address these three issues, but they are generally limited in flexibility and in the number of data elements that can be shared among applications. Products such as SAS (www.sas.com) and SAP Crystal Solutions (www.sap.com) may be more viable solutions for a smaller healthcare organization with limited information systems resources. Another approach is to build a system from scratch, but this takes years and deep pockets, and results in—at best—another HIS standard to add to the endless list of standards.

Properly implemented, a data warehouse can provide the transparency, adherence to standards, and adaptability in our perfect system of the future. To the extent that a healthcare IT shop has access to and documentation on the database underlying the data warehouse, there is transparency. Constructing new reports is a matter of locating the relevant parameters in the documented database and manipulating it with appropriate reporting tools. Standards, including vocabulary, definitions, data structures, and operating systems, are integral to the design of a data warehouse. Similarly, performance, in terms of minimizing both query response time and the effect on transactional applications, is a feature of the properly implemented data warehouse.

A data warehouse, like the other options available to CIOs, has both benefits and liabilities. As typically implemented, a significant limitation of the data warehouse is that it serves as the basis for reporting and decision support, but not for transactional applications. In other words, the transparency is primarily useful for lightweight decision support applications that feed on the data warehouse. Transaction-based applications that must both read and write to a database are not supported.

Furthermore, standards must be selected carefully during the design of the data warehouse to avoid a confusing mix of standards that hinders system maintenance and prevents direct comparison of the healthcare enterprise performance with national and international benchmarks. In addition, the performance of the typical data warehouse can only approximate real time, in that data are at best updated every quarter-hour. More commonly, however, it is updated every night to minimize the negative impact on the source data applications. And, to add to the list of unmet challenges, most healthcare enterprises have yet to even consider the implications of interfacing with genomic and proteomic data from regional, national, and international centers. Clearly, there will be no shortage of work for healthcare CIOs for the foreseeable future.

Evolutionary Pressures

The economic and legislative pressures on the healthcare enterprise to provide quality healthcare at lower cost and with fewer resources have intensified. As costs shift from third-party payers to patients, the business of healthcare has begun to look like business in any other industry. Hospitals that provide superior outcomes, contain costs, and maintain profitability will thrive at the expense of less fit institutions. CEOs in healthcare organizations are becoming increasingly aware of quality and performance management initiatives that have had a positive effect on the bottom line of businesses in other industries.

Some of the pressure on the modern healthcare enterprise is from performance-promoting organizations such as the Joint Commission, Centers for Medicare and Medicaid Services (CMS), the Agency for Healthcare Research and Quality (AHRQ), and the International Organization for Standardization (ISO). Most of these organizations promote the use of key performance indicators (KPIs) to help management more effectively direct the use of their organization's resources, maximize patient safety, promote clinical best practices, and increase patient satisfaction.

The Joint Commission's ORYX initiative includes performance indicators as part of its accreditation process. The organization defines performance in terms of outcome parameters, including efficiency, appropriateness, availability, timeliness, effectiveness, continuity, safety, and respect for caring. Its international equivalent, Joint Commission International (JCI), promotes quality standards that reflect practices outside of the United States.

CMS offers certification to healthcare organizations with quality initiatives that are planned, systematic, comprehensive, and ongoing. Specific, predetermined indicators and benchmarks form the basis of CMS performance indicators. AHRQ indicators cover access, utilization, cost, effectiveness, safety, timeliness, and patient-centeredness. ISO offers a process that a performance management system can follow for implementation.

Technology

Fiscal responsibility and the pressure of continuous quality improvement for healthcare IT favors a move from a disorganized system of different software packages running on different, incompatible hardware and abiding by various protocols to a seamless, organized system—and this is where the data warehouse comes in. Although it is often mistaken for an overgrown reporting system, the ideal data warehouse is a central, homogenous repository of a carefully selected subset of data from disparate, often loosely integrated applications in an organization. By virtue of this organization, the repository supports rapid data mining, report generation, and decision support.

Implementing a data warehouse is a technical challenge on several fronts, from data capture and transfer to controlling data access and handling the disposal of data. Consider that data from computers, RFID readers, bar code readers and bedside monitors must be acquired and made accessible in a way that is timely, accurate, secure, and HIPAA compliant. Furthermore, raw indicator values must be processed, filtered, and formatted before decision makers can use them as key quality indicators.

To appreciate the technological considerations and challenges inherent in implementing a data warehouse, consider the smaller and simpler clinical data repositories and data marts. A clinical data repository is a structured, systematically collected storehouse of patient-specific clinical data. These data are usually mirrored from a single clinical application but may be supplemented with data from other clinical systems. By maintaining a separate database, configured specifically to support decision analysis, the application database engine is spared computational loading, and the response time to a particular query should be improved.

Furthermore, because virtually all patient information in the host application is mirrored in the clinical data repository, complex, customized queries are possible without degrading the performance of the source applications. In addition, because the data tend to originate from one source, with little to no data manipulation, near-real-time retrieval of clinical data is possible.

Stepping up one level of complexity, a data mart contains data extracted from clinical and nonclinical applications, including summary data. In operation, a select subset of data from multiple transactional applications are checked for errors, summarized, and imported into a central database. Data marts tend to be used at the department level and are often isolated from the larger healthcare enterprise.

A data warehouse is an enterprise-wide central repository of information that reflects activity within most applications running in the enterprise. As with a data mart, a data warehouse combines data from a variety of application databases into a central database. This requires cleaning, encoding, and translating data so that analysis can be performed. Data redundancy may be intentionally built in to the data warehouse to maximize the efficiency of the underlying database engine—for example, by minimizing the number of relational tables to be joined in a report query. There are also the usual database issues to consider, such as security, data integrity, synchronization, failure recovery, and general data management.

People

Technology is necessary but insufficient for the continued evolution of the healthcare enterprise. As with prepping a seagoing vessel for a long journey, a well-provisioned and trained staff goes a long way to mitigate the risk of failure. This reliance on trained staff is recognized by the federal incentive funding under the HITECH component of the American Recovery and Reinvestment Act of 2009; meaningful-use criteria are focused on people-oriented organizational change, not technology. Creating a hospital information system that is actually used requires all stakeholders to understand the mission of the enterprise, share the vision of the administration, and have the motivation to overcome the challenges that must be addressed. However, even the best-intentioned CIO or hospital administrator is powerless to make the appropriate change without timely, accurate, and relevant information.

As many medical IT professionals discovered long ago, any technological enablers must be embraced by the user communities for the technologies to have a positive impact. Simply providing decision makers with a torrent of data through sophisticated, hi-tech graphical displays is worthless without an underlying strategy.

One such strategy is performance management. The basis of performance management is the effective use of resources, as measured by quantifying processes and outcomes using KPIs that gauge the performance of an organization in particular areas. Performance management initiatives that have been applied in healthcare and other industries include aspects of statistical process control, total quality management, customer relationship management, activity-based costing, ISO 9000/ISO 9001:2015, and knowledge management. Because performance management is a tough sell in clinically based organizations, initiatives are often better defined in terms of quality.

Knowledge management—a deliberate, systematic business optimization strategy that involves the selection, distillation, storage, organization, packaging, and communication of information—is particularly relevant to the success of a data warehouse–enabled performance management project. This strategy treats intellectual capital, including process, structures, information systems, financial relations, and intellectual properties, as a major organizational asset that can be tracked, measured, and analyzed with performance or quality indicators. (See Figure 1.3 for a map of typical knowledge management operations.) Knowledge management is practiced to some degree

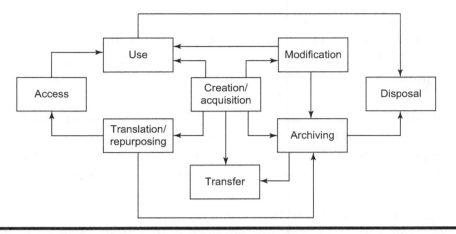

Figure 1.3 Typical knowledge management operations.

in every successful knowledge-intensive organization, including the data-driven healthcare enterprise.

Monsters

Yes, there be monsters here. However, just as the sea captains of old went forth in spite of the risks, healthcare CIOs are moving forward with data warehouse implementations. Those that succeed are prepared. They both know exactly where they're going and have a good idea of how to get there. For example, the successful CIO knows that the ideal data warehouse automatically downloads data from application databases, cleans and transforms data as necessary, and then combines them into a central database. A properly implemented data warehouse also takes care of timing issues and populates a central database in such a way as to support the most likely queries to be asked. Ideally, most data warehouse performance management efforts are begun through a lengthy requirements process; all the key users select the fields that are used to populate their most used queries. These fields are voted on before the data warehouse is built.

The successful CIO knows that most of the technical implementation challenges are related to the independently designed application database systems that rely on different data representations, unique vocabularies, and different update timings. For example, one application might represent date as "day/month/year," whereas another application uses "month/day/year." In order for the data warehouse to provide valid date information, data from one or more application databases must be translated into the representation used in the data warehouse. Only then can the data be sorted, massaged, translated, and reformatted to support data mining, discovering patterns in the data, compiling outcome statistics, or performing ad hoc queries.

Successful CIOs are also aware that variation in application update timings creates data warehouse timing and synchronization challenges. Ideally, all information entering the data warehouse represents an instant in time when all transactions are frozen and data edits and modifications are halted. In reality, even if the data are downloaded from each transactional database at the same instant, they may be out of sync because of how the applications are written. For example, one application may write data out to disc every hour, whereas a second application writes data to disc immediately after each transaction.

Variations in application vocabularies present unique challenges as well. A central issue in data warehouse design is that there are several vocabulary standards available for use in the central database and query engines. SNOMED, DICOM, ICD-10, and UMLS all have issues related to completeness and applicability to particular clinical and nonclinical domains.

In assessing the many challenges associated with implementing a data warehouse, it is tempting to focus on the technology. After all, technology is logical, controllable, and eventually works, given sufficient time and effort. However, as you'll note in the accounts contained in the following chapters, the greatest challenges are related to people, not technology. The success of any data warehouse implementation will be limited to the degree that your people and the processes are in place to work with the system. Because there will always be doubts in the minds of the men and women who do the heavy lifting, leadership, whether taking your team across uncharted waters or through a data warehouse implementation, is the greatest determinant of success.

References

1. Gartner 2005. Gartner Says More than 50 Percent of Data Warehouse Projects Will Have Limited Acceptance or Will Be Failures through 2007. Gartner Newsroom. February 24, 2005. Available at: http://www.gartner.com/newsroom/id/492112.

2. Goasduff, L. 2015. Gartner Says Business Intelligence and Analytics Leaders Must Focus on Mindsets and Culture to Kick Start Advanced Analytics. Gartner Newsroom. September 15, 2015. Available at: http://www.gartner.com/newsroom/id/3130017.
3. Schade, S. 2016. Getting to Stage 7 on the HIMSS Analytics EMR Adoption Model a Big Leap from Stage 6. Healthcare IT News, December 12, 2016. Available at: http://www.healthcareitnews.com/blog/getting-stage-7-himss-analytics-emr-adoption-model-big-leap-stage-6.

Chapter 2

Data Warehouses as Feeders to Data Analytics and Business Intelligence: The Good, the Great, the Bad, and the Ugly

Bryan Bergeron

Contents

Introduction

When exploring new lands, medieval captains replenished their store of rations and, if need be, rounded up a few volunteers to replace sailors who fell overboard during a storm or were lulled away from the ship by sirens and drowned. This one-stop-shopping approach was convenient for the captain, but it did have one down side in that the reluctant recruits often weren't fluent in the captain's native tongue. The first order of business was then to establish a common terminology for peeling potatoes, swabbing the deck, hoisting the mainsail, and the like. This common data dictionary, if you will, was necessary for the efficient operation of the ship.

Similarly, in a data warehouse initiative, in order to share a common vision, everyone on the IT implementation team has to agree on terminology. For the purpose of this book, the relationships between the data warehouse, analytics, business intelligence (BI), and decision support are illustrated in Figure 2.1. As shown in the figure, administrative, clinical, and claims data from a variety of applications and databases are processed and stored in the data warehouse. Data from the data warehouse are then fed to analytics and BI applications.

Analytical applications, referred to as *data analytics*, perform various statistical and mathematical operations on data. The output of these applications is fed to both BI and decision support applications. Analytics directly support real-time and prospective decision support. BI applications, in contrast, include query and reporting tools, such as dashboards. BI applications are used retrospectively to identify and help visualize patterns, such as historical trends in data.

Whether real time or retrospective, the main purpose of developing a data warehouse is to support administrative, clinical, and research decision making. Better decisions translate to cost savings, time savings, fewer

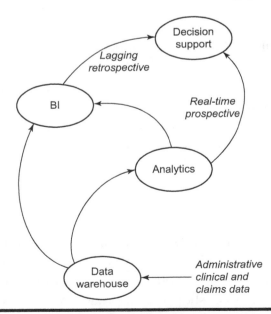

Figure 2.1   Relationships between the data warehouse, analytics, BI, and decision support.

mistakes, and, ultimately, higher-quality patient care. The three user silos of decision support have somewhat different needs. Administrators, in general, are concerned with staffing, logistics, and the bottom line. Clinicians leverage real-time support for diagnosing and treating patients. Researchers look at historical administrative data to reveal past successes and failures in providing quality patient care in order to modify and create clinical guidelines.

Each of these silos of users takes a slightly different approach to data analytics. Even so, each group must support the process of inspecting, cleaning, transforming, and modeling data. The degree of urgency is of course dependent on the user. For example, a physician entering an order for a drug must have feedback within seconds as to whether the drug has the potential to interact with medications already in the patient's bloodstream. Administrators, on the other hand, are generally concerned with longer-term activities, such as when to reorder surgical supplies or at what intervals to replenish the formularies.

Given this understanding of how the terms *analytics, business intelligence*, and *decision support* are related, let's discusses the potential good, great, bad, and ugly of a data warehouse as a feeder to BI and data analytical applications and methods. For the following discussion, let's put on our administrator's hats and look at physician productivity.

Physician Productivity: A Matter of Perspective

One of the pillars of clinical cost containment is assessing physician productivity. Overspending, inconsistency in treatment, errors, and suboptimal results can be due to a poorly performing physician. But what is poor performance? From an administrator's perspective, productivity often translates to cost-effectiveness—how one physician compares to another, or to a national average, in terms of salary requirements, medical supply costs, length-of-stay costs, and other physician-directed expenditures. From a clinical director's perspective, performance is usually framed in terms of the quality of care delivered, based on a physician's adherence to, or deviation from, established clinical guidelines, whether intentional or due to carelessness or ignorance. From a patient's perspective, productivity is often understood in terms of the value delivered—freedom from whatever malady ailed them, through procedures performed quickly, with empathy, and at reasonable cost.

While these definitions come from vastly different perspectives, they all share concepts of increased physician accountability, increased quality and cost control, and a disdain for inconsistency, errors, and suboptimal results. Given these parameters, how does a data warehouse compare with the alternative of piecemeal data source feeds for analytics and BI applications?

The Good

At the simplest level, a data warehouse can be configured to support multiple perspectives of physician productivity simultaneously. For example, a physician's track record for correct diagnoses, as well as clinical outcomes, as measured by patient survival and complication rates, can be extracted from the EHR and stored in the data warehouse. Overheads, in terms of money, time, and hospital bed occupancy, can similarly be extracted from admission–discharge–transfer (ADT) and other systems and made available to both analytic and BI applications. Without a data dictionary, these and other variables would not be processed and immediately available for inclusion in an expert system, simulation, or other decision support application. Reports would be weeks, if not months, behind the actual events—far too long to use the data to make meaningful changes in process.

The Great

Perhaps the greatest advantage of having all relevant patient, physician, and hospital data cleaned and ready to be fed to an appropriate algorithm or dashboard is relatively stable and reliable results. With myriad data sources to deal with, the odds of error are increased, especially if cleaning and transformation operations are manually directed and application specific. A data warehouse greatly improves the accessibility and quality of the data that forms the basis for decision support.

The Bad

If there's a bad category associated with the use of a data warehouse to feed analytical and BI applications, it has to be physician behavior and resistance to being monitored on a daily basis. While this isn't a technology issue, all of the technologies related to the system provide greater insights into physician behavior. To physicians who don't buy into the Orwellian monitoring, the data warehouse may represent a technology they'd rather not have at their hospital.

The Ugly

Related to the bad category, the primary ugly aspect of the data warehouse system depicted in Figure 2.1 is the potential for physicians to game the system. Physicians may cut back on the care of severely ill patients for fear of worsening their efficiency scores, for example. All in all, a minor ugly.

Summary Judgment

A data warehouse feeder to a BI and analytics engine is a powerful combination. Whether the basis of BI or analytics, or both, the cleaned, synchronized data in a data warehouse present a cleaner, easier-to-access store that can be used as the basis for decision support.

Chapter 3

Enterprise Environment

Hamad Al-Daig

Contents

Introduction

Change is an inevitable fact of life for people, technologies, and organizations. In today's complex world, change occurs at such an accelerated rate that people and organizations have to constantly rethink the way they use information and enable technologies to do business. To succeed, organizations have to focus an increasing amount of their energy on the analysis and management of information. This chapter provides an overview of the King Faisal Specialist Hospital and Research Centre (KFSH&RC) up-to-date enterprise environment from an operational prospective, including clinical load, IT infrastructure, and organizational structure.

KFSH&RC is a modern, multisite, tertiary-care referral hospital that provides the highest international standard of healthcare. Patients include members of the Saudi Arabian Royal Family, dignitaries, and patient referrals from throughout the Kingdom of Saudi Arabia. The hospital was founded in 1975 in Riyadh, the capital of Saudi Arabia (Figure 3.1). It is the first hospital in the Middle East recognized by HIMSS as a Stage 7 hospital for its electronic health record (EHR) adoption level. KFSH&RC received the 2011 Digital Excellence Award from the Ministry of Communications and Technology of Saudi Arabia for the enriched contents and services (14 e-services) provided through the KFSH&RC web portal.

KFSH&RC is accredited by the Joint Commission on International Accreditation (JCIA) for its high international standard of healthcare delivery. It is also accredited by the College of American Pathologists (CAP) for pathology and laboratory medicine. In 2011, KFSH&RC achieved ISO 27001 Information Security Management certification for its robust IT security infrastructure—a certification that has been renewed regularly since then. Furthermore, as detailed in this book, KFSH&RC is one of the first hospitals in the Middle East to embark on a data warehouse project.

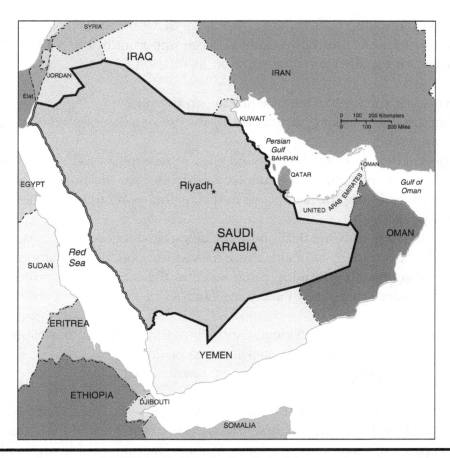

Figure 3.1 Location of KFSH&RC, Riyadh, Saudi Arabia.

Staffing

KFSH&RC started its journey as a 120-bed, single-site hospital staffed by about 500 employees. Over the years, it has grown to its current size with two major sites, 1,400 beds, and a multinational base of more than 14,000 employees.

Clinical services are enriched by the expertise of highly qualified professionals from 78 countries, with the majority from Europe and North America. For example, there are more than 3,300 nurses primarily from the United States, Canada, the United Kingdom, Ireland, Australia, New Zealand, the Philippines, and South Africa. Of the 1,500-plus physicians, about half are consultants, with the balance consisting of specialists, residents, and fellows. There are 128 residency and fellowship training programs, involving 320 residents and fellows.

The cosmopolitan staff brings a vast array of work, socioeconomic, and corporate experience to the institution. More importantly, the staff continually strives for excellence by focusing on its mission:

- Providing the best tertiary healthcare in the region
- Establishing standards of excellence for the practice of medicine in Saudi Arabia
- Conducting scientific and applied clinical research—and cooperating with other specialized institutions worldwide—to develop therapies that improve the level of healthcare in the region, particularly in the medical subspecialties
- Cooperating with medical and educational institutions to increase the level of awareness of healthcare issues in the patient population
- Providing health education programs and the training of Saudi nationals in order to ensure an adequate number of qualified specialists are available
- Providing accredited residency and fellowship programs for Saudi physicians in order for them to contribute to healthcare
- Publishing periodicals and scientific medical journals

KFSH&RC is regarded as the leader in serving populations with both specialized healthcare and high service needs in the Middle East. The positioning of the institution in Saudi Arabia's national healthcare market is illustrated in Figure 3.2, which shows that the National Guard hospital and military hospitals are the only other institutions in Saudi Arabia catering to similar patient populations. However, some of the Ministry of Health's (MOH) new medical sites compete for the same patient population. The security forces hospital and some university hospitals cater to patients with specialized healthcare needs but only moderate service needs. Government polyclinics and private clinics serve populations with general healthcare and moderate service needs. General hospitals and private hospitals cater to patients with high service needs but only general healthcare requirements.

Because of KFSH&RC's positioning among other healthcare institutions in Saudi Arabia, both patient and referring physician expectations are very high regarding the quality of care and the hospital's ability to address specialized healthcare needs. Moreover, the educated patient population increasingly demands more specialized services at the same or a higher level of quality. KFSH&RC's ability to satisfy these demands in a fiscally responsible manner

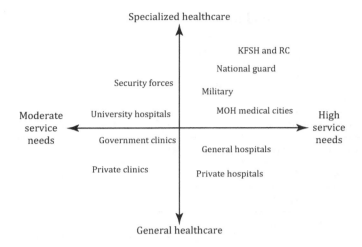

Figure 3.2   Perception map showing the relationship of KFSH&RC with other health-care providers in the region, stratified by service need and degree of specialization.

is an ongoing challenge similar to that faced by hospitals in the European Union and United States.

The real challenge is the increase in the capabilities of competing hospitals as well as the new tertiary-care hospitals built and supported by the MOH with similar capabilities to provide wider choices of care for its citizenry. Facing this challenge responsively requires a multidimensional approach that includes patient outreach, clinical and administrative staff training, and clinical and information-handling technologies. The impetus behind the data warehouse project is to provide clinical and administrative staff with the technological leverage they need to analyze vast amounts of data in a way that facilitates timely and accurate decision making.

Clinical Load

Average annual patient referral is more than 44,500 patients, with approximately 60% accepted for treatment. Tables 3.1 and 3.2 illustrate the magnitude and nature of clinical load from 2007 to 2011. The average length of stay is 10.52 days, the bed occupancy rate is 89%, and the hospital handles more than 829,000 outpatient clinic visits annually.

KFSH&RC's core competencies are in the area of tertiary care, as reflected by the caseload by type, as shown in Figures 3.3 through 3.5. Recently,

Table 3.1   Clinical Load in 2011

Clinical Load 2011	
Beds (inpatient)	1,046
Day beds	350
Patients accepted	26,751
Inpatient admission (excl. newborns)	32,909
Discharges (excl. newborns)	32,783
Average length of stay	10.68
Average daily census	889
Bed occupancy rate (percent)	89
Outpatient clinic visits	920,547
Emergency department visits	89,218
Operating room procedures	18,107
Day surgery procedures	6,473
Laboratory tests	8,549,021
Radiology procedures	270,491

cardiac catheterizations and cardiac surgeries account for approximately half of the caseload. Most of the remaining caseload are new cancer cases.

The significant cardiac caseload is handled by the King Faisal Heart Institute (KFHI), a tertiary cardiac care delivery center with clinical sections devoted to adult cardiology, pediatric cardiology, cardiac surgery, and cardiac surgical critical care. KFHI is fully capable and committed to meeting the growing needs of Saudi Arabian patients for all types of cardiovascular diseases by providing team-oriented, evidence-based practice. Advanced informatics systems, cutting-edge research, and advanced education are also cornerstones of KFHI.

Bone marrow and renal transplants have increased considerably since 2000. KFSH&RC ranks at the top among the 275 centers worldwide that perform bone marrow transplants. In addition, the number of kidney, liver, pancreas, heart, lung, and bone transplants performed in 2010 reached 671, which amounts to almost two transplants every 24 h.

KFSH&RC has the largest cancer facility in the Gulf region, treating 40% of all registered cancer cases in Saudi Arabia, or nearly 3,000 new

Table 3.2   Clinical Load in 2016

Clinical Load 2016	2016
Beds (inpatient)	1,127
Day beds	435
Patients accepted	17,486
Inpatient admission (excl. newborns)	29,971
Discharges (excl. newborns)	29,968
Average length of stay	12.41
Average daily census	1,090
Bed occupancy rate (percent)	98.24
Outpatient clinic visits	1,083,438
Emergency department visits	88,948
Operating room procedures	210,930
Day surgery procedures	6,387
Laboratory tests	26,404,247
Radiology procedures	115,081

cases every year. The five core programs of the Cancer Centre are in the areas of breast cancer, lymphoma, sarcoma, stereotactic radiosurgery, and intensity-modulated radiation therapy (IMRT).

The Cyclotron and Radiopharmaceuticals department produces a variety of radioisotopes and diagnostic and therapeutic radiopharmaceuticals as well as supporting 40 nuclear medicine centers in Saudi Arabia. The department also supplies radiopharmaceuticals to most of the MOH hospitals in the Gulf region. Research is focused on the areas of cancer, genetics, cardiovascular diseases, environmental health, and infectious diseases. Research results have been published in major medical journals and have resulted in numerous patents and invention disclosures.

IT Infrastructure

The Healthcare Information Technology Affairs (HITA) department is the driving force behind the hospital's innovations in healthcare. The focus of HITA is leveraging technology to improve the quality of patient care and

Procedure	2000	2001	2002	2003	2004	2005	
Cardiac surgeries	1776	1737	1761	1639	1661	1449	
Cardiac catheterizations	2874	3174	2996	2434	2722	2781	
New cancer cases	2736	2663	2617	2862	2812	2893	
Bone marrow transplants	134	141	178	181	206	223	
Liver transplants	0	5	8	9	32	29	
Renal transplants	44	63	91	104	111	127	
Lung transplants	1	0	0	1	3	3	
Pancreas transplants	0	0	0	0	1	2	
Heart transplants	2	3	2	6	5	7	

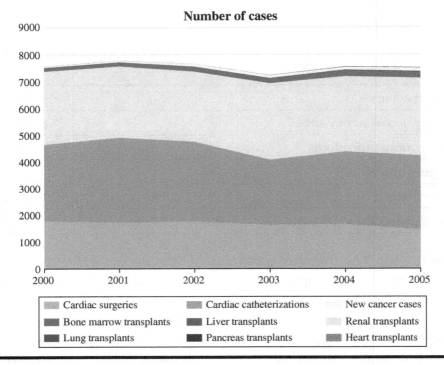

Figure 3.3   Cases by area, 2000–2005.

satisfaction. Achieving these goals has required the HITA to reinvent itself over time, shifting focus to suit the needs of the hospital and the maturity of available technologies. As illustrated in Figure 3.6, HITA began in the mid-1970s with a focus on ready-made or shrink-wrapped software applications and hardware solutions. A decade later, with the increased availability of affordable development tools, HITA invested heavily in homegrown development.

With the maturation of the healthcare informatics market in the early 1990s—including the availability of off-the-shelf clinical systems—HITA

Procedure	2006	2007	2008	2009	2010	2011	
Cardiac surgeries	1234	1346	1365	1297	1353	1366	
Cardiac catheterizations	2632	2794	2772	2110	2141	6618	
New cancer cases	2493	2416	2576	2514	2469	2506	
Bone marrow transplants	239	216	264	264	312	277	
Liver transplants	36	36	41	46	46	89	
Renal transplants	141	145	152	137	145	170	
Lung transplants	3	0	0	1	7	12	
Heart transplants	12	12	19	14	19	15	
Bone	0	0	0	0	12	27	

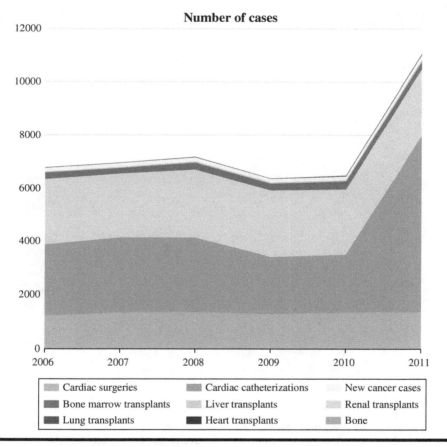

Figure 3.4   Cases by area, 2006–2011.

focused on integrating best-of-breed solutions. While this approach provided department-wide solutions to clinical and administrative decision support and specialized function support, the software and hardware solutions were fragmented. As a result, formulating an overall picture of the hospital operation was problematic. Beginning in 2000 and extending to the present, the focus of HITA has been on enterprise-wide, integrated solutions.

Procedure	2016	2015	2014	2013	2012
Cardiac surgeries	2692	2768	2659	2658	2876
Cardiac catheterizations	7027	7498	6755	6435	6611
New cancer cases	1607	1461	1487	1694	1472
Bone marrow transplants	380	323	308	342	336
Liver transplants	134	124	124	115	102
Renal transplants	395	369	306	283	262
Lung transplants	16	19	11	18	13
Pancreas transplants	10	7	2	1	0
Heart transplants	28	30	26	15	19

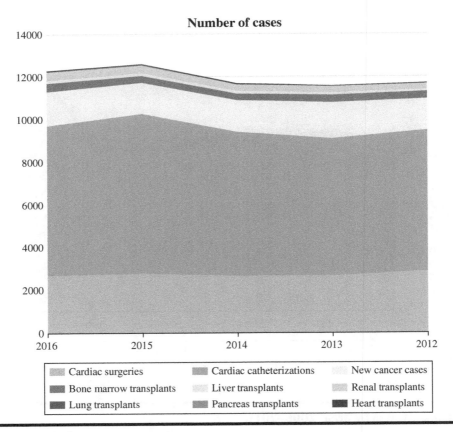

Figure 3.5   Cases by area, 2012–2016.

The data warehouse project is a prime example of the hospital's current focus on integrated solutions. However, before considering the data warehouse in depth, it is worth taking a moment to understand the primary IT infrastructure. These elements, which range from applications to storage and network architecture, are outlined here.

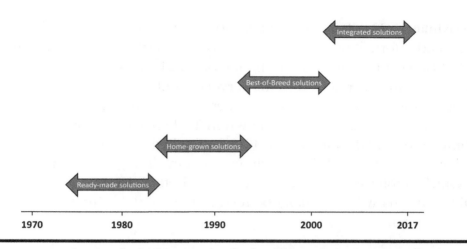

Figure 3.6   Eras of technological innovation by healthcare information technology affairs.

Applications

The cornerstones of the hospital's application suite are the Integrated Clinical Information System (ICIS) and Enterprise Resource Planning (ERP) system. ICIS is based on the Health Network Architecture (HNA) Millennium suites from the Cerner Corporation. KFSH&RC has implemented the Person Management, Scheduling, Surgery, Radiology, Laboratory, Computerized Physician Order Entry (CPOE), Pharmacy, Operating Room, Emergency Medicine, and Medical Records modules. Implementation of the Pharmacy, Surgery, Emergency Medicine, and Medical Records modules alone involved approximately 5,000 database tables of patient data, physician order, and test results.

The hardware requirements imposed by ICIS and the ERP system are addressed by a three-tier architecture system based on two IBM P590 servers attached to an IBM DS8000 SAN disk storage system with more than 50 TB of storage capacity. This configuration provides high performance, availability, reliability, adaptability, and a high degree of data integrity.

ERP operations are provided by an Oracle Integrated Financial and Material Management System built around Inventory, Purchasing, Order Management, General Ledger, Accounts Payable, and Fixed Assets—all modules from the Oracle Corporation. A homegrown personnel and payroll system that manages employee, salary, and benefits-related information has been replaced by Oracle's human resource (HR) management application. The Integrated Financial and Material Management System relies on approximately 32,000 database tables to capture logistic, financial, and HR-related information. The system is hosted on two IBM P770 servers in a LPAR (logical partitioning) configuration. A 21 TB IBM DS8000 SAN disk storage system is connected to the servers via fiber.

Many other stand-alone systems cater to departmental needs. A partial, updated list of these systems is shown in Table 3.3. Only some of these systems have an HL7 interface to ICIS for feeding patient, order, and result information, and few of the nonclinical systems have custom interfaces to the Oracle application. Because of these and other limitations, many of these clinical systems will eventually be replaced by modules from either ICIS or the ERP system.

Network

The network infrastructure is based on a 10 Gbps fiber-cabled backbone, connecting data center core switches with enterprise distribution switches. All hospital buildings are redundantly fiber connected to the backbone through CISCO 3750 distribution switches that in turn provide network connectivity to building floors. In total, the network consists of the following:

■ Two Nexus 7000 Switches
■ Four Nexus 5000 Switches
■ Six Cisco 6500 Switches

Table 3.3 Stand-Alone Departmental Systems

Medical Systems	*Nonmedical Systems*
Picture archival and communication system (PACS)	Patient billing system
Cardiovascular solution (Apollo CardioStar)	Contact center
Nursing scheduling system (One-Staff)	Document management (EMC)
Medication dispensing (Pyxis and Scriptpro)	Quality assurance
Dictation and transcription food and nutrition (CBord)	Social services
Patient acceptance and eligibility	
On-call system	
Tumor registry (C/Net)	

- 450 Cisco 3750 switches for building distribution and access
- Network ports providing a link bandwidth of 100 Mbps and 1 Gbps
- 15,000 wired access points
- 1,000 wireless access points, with provision for 4,000 wireless devices

Citrix

A Citrix environment allows us to deliver applications and updates to all networked PCs with speed, security, and the flexibility of centralized management. The Citrix application delivery infrastructure reflects the convergence of selected networking, security, and management technologies required for end-to-end delivery of applications on demand. The infrastructure includes three Citrix farms on one hundred Dell servers in physical and virtual platforms.

Backup System

The enterprise backup system is based on IBM's enterprise solution that includes an IBM Automated Enterprise Backup Library containing 12 high-performance, fiber-connected tape drives. An IBM Tivoli Storage Management system provides full and incremental data backup for critical clinical data. IBM ProtecTIER® Deduplication solutions, featuring HyperFactor® data deduplication technology, provide enterprise-class performance, scalability, and data integrity.

Active Directory

User sign-on, automated user access, and centralized management is supported by a Microsoft Active Directory (AD) utility. To maximize availability, reliability, performance, and data integrity, there are eleven AD domain controllers—seven in the main hospital, one in the Children's Cancer Centre, and three in the Jeddah branch. In addition to several Dell servers, eight DNS, and five Dynamic Host Configuration Protocol (DHCP) servers complete the data center infrastructure with a *configuration management and operation management* environment.

Email and Workflow Systems

A *unified communication* infrastructure combines telephony (including IP phone), paging, video conferencing, emails, instant messaging, and voice data communication using a single unified platform. As part of this project, KFSH&RC changed its email platform from IBM Lotus Notes to Microsoft Outlook, hosted in Microsoft Exchange servers on a fully virtualized environment using VMware vSphere 5.

Application Development Environment

The IBM WebSphere platform was the foundation for in-house application development. This environment provided developers with a common web portal and single sign-on capabilities. WebSphere system components are hosted on several fully configured Dell servers.

Data Warehouse

The data warehouse system is designed to support clinical and administrative decision making. The system components are hosted on five fully configured Dell servers attached to a Dell Compellent SAN disk storage turbo model with fiber-attached disks. Details of the configuration and specifications of the data warehouse components are covered in later chapters.

E-Services

In conjunction with e-government initiatives of Saudi Arabia, KFSH&RC made the following e-services available to its patient population and employees:

1. Online appointment viewing
2. Appointments services (postponing appointments and cancelling appointments)
3. Getting medical reports
4. Ordering medication refills
5. Contacting patient relations
6. Medical supplies refills

7. Social services requests
8. Modifying personal information
9. Sick leave verification
10. Applying for residency and fellowships
11. Applying for quality and patient safety workshops
12. Treatment orders

Open Source Utilization

KFSH&RC uses Red Hat Linux Open Source OS for its strength in stability, security, flexibility, and robustness in the following areas:

■ Cerner P2Sentinel auditing software
■ ERP Discoverer
■ ERP web services
■ Virtual tape library
■ External DNS management
■ EMC Documentum
■ In-house development

Virtualization and Cloud Computing

To optimize IT operation and foster a green environment, KFSH&RC is reducing the footprint of bulk hardware and its operational expenses by investing heavily in virtualization using VMware vSphere 5 Enterprise Plus on a Dell Blade Server Series M710 and Dell Compellent SAN SC 4. Virtualization has paved the way for a cloud computing environment.

The cloud computing environment runs on VMware vCloud Director 1.5 to manage the IT infrastructure and data center assets with dynamic provisioning of IT services such as *Software as a Service* (SaaS) and *Infrastructure as a Service* (IaaS). A public cloud serves patients and external communities.

Disaster Recovery

A physical disaster recovery infrastructure for all IT services ensures business continuity with high system availability in any disaster situation. The hospital uses VMware Site Recovery Manager (SRM 5.0) along with SAN-to-SAN replication and enterprise SAN storage architecture, which use peer-to-peer, high-speed fiber optic connectivity.

Mobility

In order to go green, KFSH&RC instituted mobility solutions and distributed iPads to executives and senior management so they may have paperless meetings. It also distributed more than 9,000 smartphones to replace the paging system and provide a mobile computing platform.

Organization Structure

KFSH&RC is a multi-entity, having one corporate and two branch entities—a branch in Riyadh, the capital city of Saudi Arabia, and another in Jeddah, the second largest city in the Kingdom. The organizational structure can be characterized as Morgan's "Bureaucracy with Project Teams and Task Forces." Under the supervision of a board of directors, the minister of health serves as the chairman and the chief executive officer (CEO) as secretary general of the board. Current executive management is headed by a CEO who reports to the chairman of the board and is assisted by a chief operating officer (COO) for each of the two branches, as well as by a chief financial officer (CFO), chief administrative officer (CAO), and chief information officer (CIO).

The COO of each branch oversees five main sectors: Medical and Clinical Affairs (MCA), Administrative Affairs, Academic and Training Affairs, Nursing Affairs, and the Research Center. These five executive directors are in turn assisted by deputy executive directors, departmental heads, and chairmen. The high-level organizational chart is shown in Figure 3.7.

Medical and Clinical Affairs

MCA is the largest operational division. As such, MCA generates more data and consumes more information than any other operational division. Due to this unique position, the executive management assigned ownership of the data warehouse to MCA.

The medical division consists of seventeen medical departments, three medical units, the King Faisal Cancer Centre, the KFHI, Environmental Health and Infection Control, and Health Outreach. The medical departments, units, and entities under the MCA leadership are listed in Table 3.4.

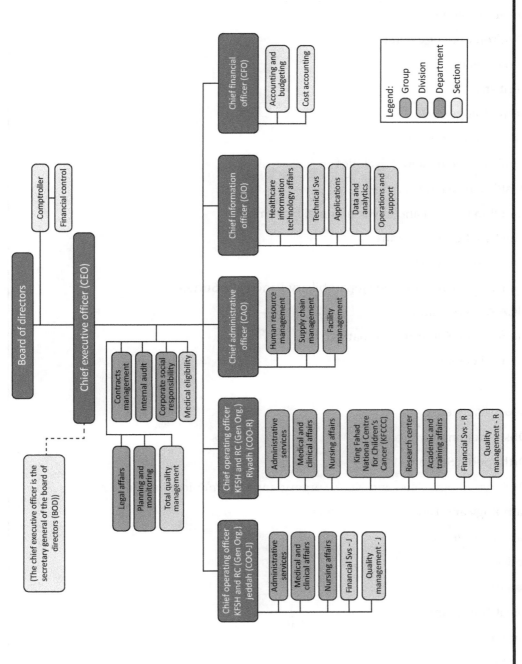

Figure 3.7 Organizational chart.

Table 3.4   Medical Departments Managed by Medical and Clinical Affairs

Medical Departments Managed by MCA
Anesthesiology
Children Cancer Center
Clinical Services
Dentistry
Dermatology
Emergency Medicine
Family Medicine and Polyclinics
Health Outreach Services
Infection Control and Environmental Health
King Faisal Cancer Centre
King Faisal Heart Institute
Liver Transplantation and Hepatobiliary-Pancreatic Surgery
MCA Administration
Medical and Clinical Informatics
Medical Genetics
Medicine
Neurosciences
Obstetrics and Gynecology
Orthopedic Surgery
Otolaryngology, Head and Neck Surgery, and Communication Science
Pathology and Laboratory Medicine
Patient Services
Pediatrics
Radiology
Renal Transplant Unit
Surgery
Urology

Table 3.5   Service Areas Covered by Nursing Affairs

Nursing Affairs Service Areas
Home care
Family care
Palliative care
Perioperative
Cardiovascular
Maternal child
Emergency care
Medical surgical
Adult and children's cancer
Ambulatory care
critical care—oncology
Student education
Nursing education
Recruitment
Patient education
Support services
Nursing informatics

Nursing Affairs has more than 3,300 nursing practitioners providing culturally sensitive nursing care. Nursing Affairs provides comprehensive services in the areas listed in Table 3.5.

The Clinical Services Division under MCA comprises several medical and technical departments, as listed in Table 3.6. The staff within the Clinical Services Division is composed of an array of competent and varied professionals who work in teams to provide patient care.

The Patient Services Division under MCA supports the delivery of high-quality healthcare by providing patient services such as psychosocial support and counseling, which can help patients by eliminating obstacles that might hinder the delivery or benefits of medical services. Departments under the Patient Service Division are

■ Appointments
■ Case Management

Table 3.6   Medical and Technical Departments under the Clinical Services Division of the MCA

Departments under the Clinical Services Division
Ambulance Services
Anesthesia Auxiliary
Clinical Engineering
Dental Laboratory
Neurophysiology Laboratory
Nutrition Services
Orthotics and Prosthetics Services
Speech and Language Pathology
Ophthalmology Services
Pharmacy Services
Physical Therapy
Radiation Therapy
Radiology Services
Respiratory Care Services
Sleep Medicine Unit

- Social Services
- Medical Records
- Nutrition

Academic and Training Affairs

Academic and Training Affairs (ATA) provides advanced education and training for the healthcare professionals in the following areas:

- Residency
- Training and development
- Continuing medical education
- Fellowship
- Life support
- Health science library

- Publication office
- Photographics

Research Center

The Research Center of the hospital is a center of excellence in five areas of biomedical research: cancer, genetics, cardiovascular diseases, environmental health, and infectious diseases. The center is staffed by more than 300 research scientists, clinicians, postdoctoral fellows, and technicians working in the following six departments:

- Biological and Medical Research
- Biomedical Physics
- Cyclotron and Radiopharmaceuticals
- Biostatistics, Epidemiology, and Scientific Computing
- Comparative Medicine
- Genetics

The Research Center engages in joint research programs with other centers in the United States, United Kingdom, France, Germany, Japan, Morocco, Canada, and Australia, as well as centers in Saudi Arabia. The Research Center has generated more than 800 research papers in the past six years.

Administrative Affairs

Administrative Affairs provides oversight of administrative and support service resources for all departments. The following divisions and departments are under the leadership of Administrative Affairs.

- Talent Management (corporate level)
- Performance and Reward Management (corporate level)
- Job Evaluation and Compensation (corporate level)
- Human Resource Policy and Planning (corporate level)
- Personnel Department (branch level)
- Employment Department (branch level)

Financial Affairs

Financial Affairs oversees all financial matters at the corporate and branch levels for KFSH&RC at large. The following divisions and departments are under the leadership of Financial Affairs.

- Accounting and Budgeting (corporate level)
- Cost Accounts (corporate level)
- Business Advisory (corporate level)
- Financial Services (branch level)
- General Accounting (branch level)
- Budgeting and Financial Reporting (branch level)
- Disbursement Department (branch level)
- Revenue Department (branch level)

Facility Management Group

The Facility Management Group (FMG) is in charge of utilities and maintenance as well as engineering services. Areas of responsibility range from water treatment and emergency electrical services to monitoring the pneumatic tube delivery system.

Healthcare Information Technology Affairs

HITA is a project-oriented cost center that provides IT services to all other departments within the hospital, as well as acting as a driver for the direction of IT for the institution. HITA is headed by the CIO, who reports directly to the CEO of corporate executive management. HITA plays a key role in operations and interfaces frequently with the board of directors, the CEO, executive management, and the clinical community. The organizational chart for HITA is shown in Figure 3.8.

HITA, comprised of 380 full-time employees, has two main areas of focus. The first, Application Services, involves covering systems used throughout the hospital, such as ICIS, ERP, and many other department-specific application systems. The primary goal of Application Services is to improve and streamline patient care and provide a positive patient experience. A secondary goal is to foster employee satisfaction. The second focus area, IT Infrastructure Services, provides databases, help desks, user support, computer operations, network operations, and open system support, providing tangible IT support services to assist physicians, nurses, therapists, and users at large within KFSH&RC.

The communication department of the hospital has been merged with HITA to align the voice and data services under one umbrella.

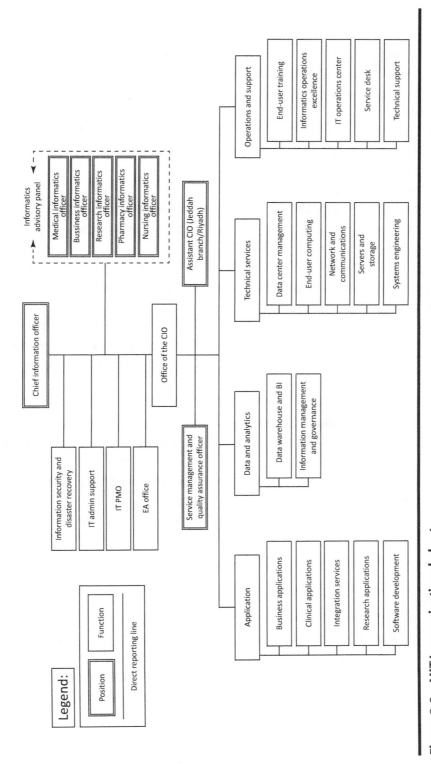

Figure 3.8   HITA organizational chart.

The strategic goals of the HITA are to provide

- Patients with access to enabling technologies that can improve their access to services, allowing them to communicate with the service providers and securely access their health information and care schedules.
- Clinicians with an integrated electronic patient record they will use as a primary resource for clinical information, documentation, and evidence.
- Staff with the information and technology they need for informed decision making and supporting hospital processes.
- Services to neighboring hospitals and community partners, and enable them to access captured patient-specific information.
- The board of directors and management with access to benchmarked information on clinical quality, outcomes, and operational performance to enhance informed decision making.
- The public with access to the hospital's measures of performance.
- IT with an infrastructure sufficiently robust to support the continuity of patient care and business operations during a time of natural or man-made disaster.

The strategic vision includes the continued development of the EHR so that it provides increased depth and breadth of clinical content and can better support decision making at the point of care. This vision reflects the hospital's transition to a more regionalized, community-based care system, and anticipates KFSH&RC's emergence as the leader in a national healthcare initiative. KFSH&RC also anticipates a shift to performance-based accountability and the development of a national EHR.

Summary

Successful organizations benefit from the deployment of technology to the extent that changes are analyzed and managed from multiple perspectives, including the proper technology, the current information system, the staff, and the structure of an organization. The data warehouse is an enabling technology that triggers significant changes in the way information is used for decision-making support at the individual and organizational levels.

The KFSH&RC healthcare enterprise has many parallels with large tertiary-care hospitals in the European Union and United States, especially in the use of IT. Most notable is that KFSH&RC decided to develop a data warehouse against a backdrop of a continually evolving suite of applications and IT initiatives.

Chapter 4

Vendor Selection and Management

Hamad Al-Daig

Contents

Introduction

Issuing a request for proposal (RFP) for equipment and services is standard practice in healthcare IT as it encourages competitive proposals from vendors. To fulfill this role, the RFP must be clear enough for vendors to understand all of the technical issues associated with the project so they can provide a reasonable solution through implementation. Another important factor in RFP development is to make the vendor selection process transparent and equitable to all participating vendors. King Faisal Specialist Hospital and Research Centre (KFSH&RC) has addressed this issue by insuring transparency in how it purchases equipment and services. The transparency extends to both vendor selection and management processes. This chapter provides an overview of RFP development, vendor selection, and management processes that were integral to the development of the data warehouse.

Background

The impetus behind the data warehouse project was the request of KFSH&RC administrators to better utilize the wealth of information being collected by the hospital's operational source systems. Senior management envisioned the data warehouse as a means of gaining the full value of its investment in clinical and business IT, transforming the KFSH&RC enterprise into a modern, knowledge-based institution, and as a means of making more informed decisions.

Although KFSH&RC's concept of the data warehouse was driven by the needs of senior management, development was owned and championed by Healthcare Information Technology Affairs (HITA). This was in contrast to the normal manner in which HITA usually operates. Typically, a department or group approaches HITA with a specific application need, such as an accounting system, and HITA works with the department to identify the technology that best fulfills their needs. The department owns the project and is responsible for training their staff and encouraging or requiring use. However, HITA owned the data warehouse development project and was insulated from interaction with the user base.

HITA's deviation from its normal mode of operation was also a variance from successful data warehouse implementations at other institutions. As detailed in later chapters, HITA's ownership of the data warehouse had serious repercussions during and following implementation. Another major issue was whether to select a packaged data warehouse solution from one of the clinical system vendors or to build one from scratch. Choosing a packaged approach had a relative certainty of success. This approach was limited, however, because the packaged solution lacked connectivity with the hospital's other 39 clinical and administrative systems, including the hospital's enterprise resource planning (ERP) system. In the end, KFSH&RC decided to develop the data warehouse from scratch and sought out a vendor with a track record of successful data warehouse development.

RFP Development

Senior members of HITA were responsible for developing the goals, objectives, and technical and functional specifications for the RFP according to the following outline:

Section I: General RFP Information

- Enterprise background information
- Objective of the RFP
- Project scope
- Proposal preparation guidelines
- Proposal evaluation criteria

Section II: Proposal Response Form

- Proposal preparation instructions
- Proposal response rules
- Proposal summary
- Vendor and project team information
- Implementation and support information
- Proposed solution(s): specifications and capabilities
- Support and warranty
- Price quotation statement: software, hardware, and professional services

Section III: Supporting Information

- Contract administration and compliance
- Technical environment and sizing information
- Performance-measuring criteria

Methodology

The RFP development methodology KFSH&RC used for the data warehouse project was different from most of the other IT projects. The first major difference, noted previously, was primary ownership by HITA. The second difference was the nature of the solution. Although the data warehouse was composed of standard, commercial components, the integrated data warehouse solution was not an off-the-shelf product like the ERP system or the clinical information system (CIS).

The standard KFSH&RC approach to developing an RFP involves an initial study phase performed with the help of an independent consultant who is tasked with identifying organizational needs and translating these needs into deliverables. These needs and deliverables form the basis for a second contract for the development of a data warehouse. However, for the data warehouse project, KFSH&RC decided to incorporate a study phase in the RFP, including a business requirement analysis, as a separate task with some qualifying strings attached (highlighted later in this chapter) in order to mitigate risk.

KFSH&RC considered having the selected contractor identify needs and translate them into solid deliverables, hoping the contractor would be more accountable and responsible than an independent consultant who may have an imprecise knowledge of what is required for an effective implementation. Furthermore, KFSH&RC considered identifying a single vendor with experience developing and delivering data warehouses for other clients, given that some of KFSH&RC's user base was unclear in terms of their ultimate needs. That is, having only a vague idea of what a data warehouse encompassed, much of KFSH&RC's staff did not know which features were critical and which ones were of limited or no value.

Critical Success Factors

A good RFP addresses the needs of the enterprise and makes certain the needs are understood by prospective vendors. Hospital management wanted a system that was intuitive, easily understood, and simple to use. In their view, the data warehouse system should support intuitive manipulation and enable users to pose questions from multiple perspectives with minimum training or potential for confusion. Furthermore, the results had to be readily interpreted. These needs were summarized in the RFP with high-level needs that specified the following overarching requirements:

- Results must be easy to understand.
- Questions/queries should be clearly defined.
- The electronic format should be standardized.
- Content should be unified for ease of vendors, conformity and adherence.
- Content must be well structured.

In more concrete, technical terms, KFSH&RC stipulated that

- The data warehouse must be accessible to users throughout the healthcare enterprise.
- The contents of the data warehouse should be independent of intermediary systems that supply data.
- The data contained in the data warehouse must be credible—that is, consistent, accurate, timely, and appropriate for decision support.
- Ad hoc requests for data must to be responsive to the needs of users.

These points were clearly identified in the RFP so that KFSH&RC could judge the vendor's responses with confidence.

RFP Development Practices

KFSH&RC's standard practice for developing an IT-related RFP includes establishing an RFP committee composed of representatives from the main stakeholders, including hospital executive management, Administrative Affairs, Financial Services, Medical and Clinical Affairs, Academic and Training Affairs, and the Research Center. The RFP development committee was responsible for creating an RFP that represented the institution's overall requirements as well as the needs of specific departments. The committee drove the RFP development process, although HITA acted as the main facilitator.

However, for historical reasons, development of the data warehouse RFP deviated significantly from this norm. For decades, executive management had wanted the hospital to be information driven and to unify reporting sources to achieve operational efficiency. The means of achieving this were delegated to HITA, whose leadership identified the data warehouse as an enabling technology in 1993. However, two of the pillar systems at the institution, the ICIS and ERP applications, had priority for HITA resources, and this forced us to delay the data warehouse project. HITA revisited the data warehouse project in 2003, under increased pressure from hospital management. Because the requirements of the hospital departments and executive management were not clearly identified nor defined, HITA management was charged with developing the RFP for the data warehouse project.

As a consequence, an RFP development committee was formed with members from HITA, with minimum input from the clinical, administrative, academic, or financial divisions. The committee consisted of HITA's chief information officer (CIO), the chief technology officer (CTO), the head of Applications Services, and a senior systems analyst. This deviation from the standard RFP development practice was the source of many problems with the data warehouse design, development, and implementation. It also resulted in an RFP that proved to be open-ended and too protective of hospital interests.

RFP Execution

The RFP for the data warehouse project was executed through a public bidding process. After HITA developed the RFP, KFSH&RC's contract management department initiated the bidding process by announcing a tender in the local newspapers. Prospective vendors purchased the RFP document from the contract management department and responded with their bid by a specified date. Participating vendors were notified about the bid opening day, at which time, the contract management department opened all the bids, making the bidding features and figures transparent to all bidders. Upon completion of the bid opening process, the contract management department transferred all the RFP responses from participating vendors to the chairman of the vendor selection committee for evaluation and selection.

Vendor Selection

KFSH&RC's vendor selection process consisted of a sequence of activities, starting with the creation of the selection committee. Key activities included

- Preparation of decision criteria
- Finalizing the schedule of events
- Review, analysis, and evaluation of RFP responses
- Identifying vendor finalists

- Organizing vendor presentations
- Primary and alternate vendor selection

As noted earlier, KFSH&RC's vendor selection committee lacked representatives from major operational areas of the hospital, who normally add significant value in the selection process. Their value in this case was limited, because users at the department level were not in a position to assess vendor responses from a functional prospective.

Scoring and Assessment Criteria

Proposals were evaluated by scoring vendor responses using rules clearly stated in the RFP. Scores were assigned for the following:

- Technical solutions offered
- Services and service levels promised
- Project approach
- Qualifications of proposed implementation and training team members
- Price
- Overall RFP response
- Vendor qualifications
- Customer references

Despite following specific scoring criteria established by the selection committee, there was so much variation in responses that an objective comparison of scores was difficult. Even with this challenge, KFSH&RC identified a frontrunner and an alternate. As a policy, KFSH&RC identify two finalist vendors for an RFP, in the event that a contract suitable to the institution cannot be negotiated with the top vendor.

Proposal Evaluation

In evaluating proposals, KFSH&RC placed the most weight on the vendors' technical capabilities, especially documented expertise in implementing a data warehouse at a comparable medical institution. The soundness of the functional aspects of the proposed solution was also heavily weighted.

Of the five vendors that originally submitted bids to participate in the development of the data warehouse project, one withdrew because they made a technical bidding error. The committee eliminated a second vendor because of their reliance on proprietary software that would have locked the institution into the vendor's solution. The remaining three vendors were invited to demonstrate their ability to successfully implement a data warehouse through discussions, presentations, and demonstration sessions.

One of the three vendors was dropped because of their inability to demonstrate technical competency and a lack of positive client references. The two finalists were reevaluated using technical and financial metrics. One of the finalists received unanimously high scores from all committee members, even though they were not the lowest bidder.

Project Award

The committee was at odds because neither of the two finalist vendors had implementation experience with a data warehouse in a hospital setting. However, the top vendor had many successful data warehouse implementation experiences in non-healthcare industries. To minimize risk to the institution, the project award was provisional, as detailed in the following section. In addition, the committee asked the top vendor to revisit their hardware, licensing, and business intelligence (BI) toolset recommendations. As a result, the vendor revised their hardware recommendations and software licensing needs and specified BI tools that were not available at the time of their initial bid. The vendor provided the selection committee with a revised quotation that reflected these changes.

Based on the recommendation of the vendor selection committee, a contract between the hospital and the vendor was formally signed. The contract provided us with the provision of withdrawing the contract if the vendor failed to demonstrate competency in the initial study phase of the contract.

Vendor Management

Outsourcing any IT implementation project requires careful vendor management. In addition to the activities surrounding RFP development and execution, there is ongoing management of the vendor relationship, such as monitoring timelines and formally accepting deliverables. Effective vendor management, which is essential to the seamless acceptance of supplies and services, translates into cost saving, reduced cost overruns, better service, and more control over the technology buying and delivery processes.

Contract

In developing the vendor contract, KFSH&RC considered the basic types at the hospital's disposal:

■ *Fixed-price or lump sum contract*: Stipulates a fixed total price for a well-defined project. To increase the effectiveness, monetary incentives may be added for meeting or exceeding specific project objectives, such as beating a delivery deadline.
■ *Cost-based contract*: Stipulates reimbursable payment based on the vendor's actual costs plus a fee representing vendor profit. Actual costs include both direct and indirect costs. Variations of cost-based contracts include
   – *Cost plus fee* or *cost plus percentage of cost*: The vendor is reimbursed for allowable costs plus a fee based on an agreed percentage of the costs. The fee varies according to the actual costs.
   – *Cost plus fixed fee*: The vendor is reimbursed for allowable costs plus a fixed fee payment based on a percentage of the estimated project costs. The fixed fee portion does not vary with actual incurred cost.
   – *Cost plus incentive fee*: The vendor is reimbursed for allowable costs and a predetermined incentive bonus, based on achievement of certain performance objectives defined in the contract.
■ *Time and materials contract*: An open-ended contract in which the full value of the agreement and the exact quantity of items or services to be delivered are not defined at the time of the contract award. Time and materials contracts increase in value as the services are being delivered.

For this project, KFSH&RC opted for a variation of a fixed-price contract. The variations, described in the following, enhanced the hospital's ability to manage the vendor and protect KFSH&RC's interests.

Payment Schedule

Because of the uncertainty with the vendor's ability to deliver, KFSH&RC established a structured payment schedule that linked payment to achievement of the following milestones:

■ *First payment*: 10% of the total contract value to be paid upon completion of an initial study and the acceptance of the associated document. Failure would have negated continuation with the project as well as the planned purchase of hardware and software required to complete the project.

- *Second payment*: 80% of the software value to be paid at the time of software delivery.
- *Third payment*: 80% of the hardware value to be paid at the time of the hardware delivery.
- *Fourth payment*: 40% of the services cost to be paid upon completion and acceptance of the design phase of the project.
- *Fifth payment*: 20% of the services cost to be paid upon completion and acceptance of the user acceptance testing (UAT) phase of the project.
- *Sixth payment*: 20% of the services cost to be paid upon completion and acceptance of the *final deployment* phase of the project, and the issuance of the project's preliminary acceptance certificate.
- *Final payment*: 10% of the total contract value to be paid to the vendor upon the presentation of a final Zakat certificate, certifying payment of all taxes required.

Unique Stance

A unique feature of the contract was the insistence that the vendor provide a functional consultant for the project—preferably a physician with previous experience in data warehouse implementation and performance management. Furthermore, this consultant's experience had to be from a large hospital in North America similar to KFSH&RC. It proved difficult for the vendor to fulfill this later condition, because very few hospitals in North America had implemented a data warehouse at that time. However, the vendor eventually succeeded in finding the appropriate candidate from the United States to lead the functional team. The candidate was a physician formally trained in medical informatics with experience implementing hospital information systems, including a clinical data warehouse for a major U.S. teaching hospital.

Study Deliverables

The study linked the first payment to deliverables assigned to the vendor's functional consultant, including the completion and documentation of an enterprise-wide needs assessment. This assessment was to include a list of key performance indicator (KPIs) and had to reflect the hospital's needs based on current as well as future data sources and applications. In addition, the vendor was required to provide a design that supported all identified KPIs possible using the available data sources. For any needs that could not be implemented due to unavailability of data sources, the vendor was required to provide clear documentation of those unavailable data sources and elements. In addition, the vendor was required to provide us with the formulas for all KPIs identified by the functional consultant.

Knowledge Transfer versus Off-Shore Development

Ensuring adequate knowledge transfer from the vendor's development team to KFSH&RC's team was key to the long-term success of the data warehouse project. However, knowledge transfer from the functional team suffered because of limited resources on KFSH&RC's side. Although KFSH&RC was able to align resources throughout implementation in the technical area, the vendor lacked resources with the required training expertise.

KFSH&RC addressed these limitations by suggesting co-development, wherein KFSH&RC's resources worked side by side with vendor resources. Unfortunately, the co-development method of knowledge transfer slowed down the vendor's development speed. To remedy this, KFSH&RC agreed to allow the vendor to develop noncritical elements of the data warehouse off-shore, at the vendor's center of excellence. Allowing off-shore development increased speed and minimized the risk of vendor cost overruns. Identifying noncritical and repetitive activities for off-shore development was difficult because KFSH&RC was inclined to use co-development for all tasks related to data warehouse implementation. The project management process was largely advanced by the vendor and then approved on a weekly or ad hoc basis by the Administrative Committee.

Outsourcing emphasized the importance of managing the vendor relationship. KFSH&RC maximized vendor accountability through participative vendor management. The vendor was encouraged to participate in managing implementation and to take an active role in KFSH&RC's administrative and executive committees. These meetings focused on

- Authorizing the vendor's work at the appropriate time
- Facilitating activities for the vendor to carry out their work
- Expediting decisions and issuing directives as needed
- Identifying, resolving, or elevating policy issues
- Performance reporting to monitor schedule and deliverables
- Performing quality checks on deliverables

KFSH&RC consistently tried to create a win–win environment by emphasizing the success of common goals.

Lessons Learned

- In outsourcing components of the data warehouse implementation, key elements of success include an effective RFP and sound vendor selection and management processes.
- Outsourcing requires flexibility in approach and methods.
- Risk of failure can be contained by a carefully constructed contract wherein failure at key milestones terminates the vendor relationship and the expense to the enterprise.
- Transparency in terms and conditions and clearly defined roles and responsibilities can be used to create a win–win environment instead of an adversarial relationship with the vendor.

Chapter 5

Development Team

Enam UL Hoque

Contents

Building a development team with the appropriate skill sets is one of the most important factors contributing to a successful data warehouse implementation. Care exercised in defining teams early on in the initiative pays dividends later in the project. This chapter, written from the perspective of the technical project manager and information system architect, provides an overview of the development team that was created for our data warehouse project, from team formulation to the assignment of roles and responsibilities.

Formulation

Because of the scarcity of uncommitted internal resources with the requisite skills, we sought to outsource components of the data warehouse project. In particular, we looked to vendors to supply personnel to complement our internal resources. At that time, most vendors with experience in implementing a data warehouse worked in fields outside of the healthcare industry. So, our choices of vendors with experience implementing a data warehouse in a large hospital setting were limited.

Faced with the acute need for skilled personnel and the realization that our employees would be saddled with update and maintenance responsibilities, we established two criteria for vendor selection. First, the vendor had to provide a functional consultant experienced in large North American hospitals similar to ours. The functional consultant was to work with us to identify and formulate the deliverables of the data warehouse. Secondly, we required the vendor's development team to transfer knowledge of all the processes of data warehouse development to our internal team so that we could maintain the system without outside support.

The vendor eventually selected for the project, Wipro of India, had great difficulty recruiting a suitable functional consultant. After a significant delay, a consultant from the United States was recruited and the project was started. Working with the vendor prior to the start of the project, we identified the resources we would supply as well as those provided by the vendor. The primary vendor resources included the following roles:

- Program manager
- Project manager
- Functional consultant
- Functional analyst
- Technical architects (two)
- Extraction, transformation, and loading (ETL) developers (four)
- Database administrator (DBA)
- Data modeler
- End user application developers (six)
- Testing engineer

The resources we supplied included

- Project manager
- Business analysts (two)
- Technical data warehouse architect
- ETL developers (four)
- DBA
- Data modeler
- Online analytical processing (OLAP) developers (three)
- Training specialist

The vendor-supplied program manager was tasked with providing high-level project oversight for the duration of the project. The skill sets of the personnel supplied by King Faisal Specialist Hospital and Research Centre (KFSH&RC) and the vendor are summarized in Table 5.1.

The vendor proposed resource loading based on the need and the project stage, as shown in Table 5.2. Vendor-supplied resources were initially projected to peak at 15 full-time equivalents (FTEs) during week 17 of the project. (See Appendix A for a Gantt of the entire project.)

Table 5.1 Skill Sets by Title of Vendor and KFSH&RC-Supplied Personnel

Title	*Skills*	*Years of Experience*
Program manager	Program management, resource and vendor management, customer management, and tools and technologies like Cognos, Informatica, Oracle, etc.	>10 years
Project manager	Cognos, Informatica, Oracle, etc.	>7 years
ETL specialists	Informatica, Oracle, MS SQL server, etc.	>5 years
OLAP specialists	Cognos, Oracle, etc.	>5 years
Functional consultant/ analysts	Hospital administrator role with exposure to large hospital in the U.S. experience in • Clinical/patient care • Business processes • Financial aspects • Requirements of senior management (e.g., KPIs)	>8 years

Table 5.2 Vendor-Proposed Resource Loading

Week	1	2	3	4	5	6	7	8	9	10	11	12	13	14	15	16	17	18	19	20	21	22	23	24	25	26	27	28	29	30	31	32
Project manager	1	1	1	1	1	1	1	1	1	1	1	1	1	1	1	1	1	1	1	1	1	1	1	1	1	1	1	1	1	1		
Functional analyst	2	2	2	2	2	2	2	2																								
Technical architects	2	2	2	2	2	2	2	2	1	1	1	1	1	1	1	1	1	1	1	1	1	1	1	1								
DBA/ETL developers									3	3	3	3	6	6	6	6	6	6	6	6	3	3	3	3	2	2	2	2	2	2	2	2
End user application developers									3	3	3	3	5	5	5	5	6	6	6	6	6	6	6	6	2	2	1	1	1	1	1	1
Testing engineers													1	1	1	1	1	1	1	1	1	1	1	1	1	1						

In comparison, we proposed relatively flat resource loading, starting with six FTEs and ramping up to eight by week 9 of the project, as shown in Table 5.3. This loading reflected the vendor's recommendation that we maintain available resources at a fixed level to ensure effective knowledge transfer from the vendor to our staff throughout the duration of the project.

Formulating a development team expressly to maximize knowledge transfer from vendor to client is common in data warehouse implementations, particularly in the healthcare industry—medical and hospital settings—where there is a shortage of data warehousing development skills. We found it more practical and economical to develop the expertise of our in-house IT staff through on-site knowledge transfer from vendor to client, than to send out personnel for training in data warehouse development. Similarly, we found that having internal staff providing postinstallation support to the data warehouse is much more economical than enlisting a vendor to do so.

At the start of the project, the vendor-supplied members of the development team consisted of a project manager, a functional consultant, a technical manager, and an ETL specialist. We contributed a functional project manager, a technical project manager, a co-technical project manager, a senior programmer analyst for ETL, and a programmer analyst for OLAP. As per the initial plan, the vendor ramped up their resources during the project to include a functional analyst, an ETL specialist, a data modeling specialist, an Oracle DBA, and two Cognos OLAP specialists. During the ramp-up period, we added two more programmer analysts in the area of Cognos OLAP.

Resource constraints continued to plague us, particularly in the DBA/data modeling and functional areas. Our resource constraints, together with the proficiency level of vendor-supplied resources, negatively impacted the knowledge transfer. Furthermore, some of the vendor's resources lacked the expertise needed in their respective technical arena, while others lacked the ability to teach or otherwise transfer their knowledge to our team. For example, the vendor's top OLAP specialist had no experience developing a curriculum, establishing learning objectives, conducting a classroom, or other skills required to train our staff effectively.

Table 5.3   KFSH&RC-Proposed Resource Loading

Week	1	2	3	4	5	6	7	8	9	10	11	12	13	14	15	16	17	18	19	20	21	22	23	24	25	26	27	28	29	30	31	32
Project manager	1	1	1	1	1	1	1	1	1	1	1	1	1	1	1	1	1	1	1	1	1	1	1	1	1	1	1	1	1	1		
Business analyst	2	2	2	2	2	2	2	2	2	2	2	2	2	2	2	2	2	2	2	2	2	2	2	2	2	2	2	2	2	2	2	2
Technical architect	1	1	1	1	1	1	1	1	1	1	1	1	1	1	1	1	1	1	1	1	1	1	1	1								
DBA/ETL developers									3	3	3	3	3	3	3	3	3	3	3	3	3	3	3	3	3	3	3	3	3	3	3	3
OLAP developers									3	3	3	3	3	3	3	3	3	3	3	3	3	3	3	3	3	3	3	3	3	3	3	3
Training specialist													1	1	1	1	1	1	1	1	1	1	1	1	1	1	1	1	1	1	1	1

Skill Set Requirements

As the demand for a data warehouse with good information is growing, the requirements for the right skill set mix in data warehouse initiatives are likewise growing. Faced with the disparate activities and tasks involved in the development of the data warehouse, we elected to create technical and functional team divisions that were jointly staffed by vendor and hospital resources according to the required skill sets.

In addition, we realized that each team must have its own roles and responsibilities in order to function well within the group dynamics that play out in any team-oriented work environment. Thus, overlap in terms of each team's skill sets was carefully looked at, and a great deal of collaboration and communication took place to ensure the alignment of roles and responsibilities were optimized to their maximum potential.

Functional Team

The functional team was tasked with establishing and meeting end user needs and expectations. Selection criteria included imagination and creativity in translating end user needs into system specification requirements. The team, consisting of three members from KFSH&RC and two from the vendor, provided the following skill sets:

- Expert-level knowledge of all clinical and medical operations
- Working-level knowledge of financial and logistic operations in a large hospital
- Expert-level knowledge of data warehouse concepts and implementation
- Ability to work closely with hospital management and administrators
- Excellent communication and facilitation skills
- Technical writing

Technical Team

The technical development team was responsible for the heavy lifting in the data warehouse project, including the development of the infrastructure. The technical development team consisted of three distinct subteams: the OLAP Development Team, the ETL Development Team, and the Data

Model/Database Development Team. The composition of these subteams is outlined as follows.

OLAP Development Team

The OLAP subteam was composed of three of our FTEs and three from the vendor. Our selection criteria for vendor-supplied personnel included

- Expert-level knowledge of data warehouse implementation
- Expert-level knowledge of the Cognos suite of business intelligence (BI) products
- At least one member experienced in training to support the knowledge transfer of OLAP development activities to our staff
- Working knowledge of our Cerner-based Integrated Clinical Information System and Oracle Financial Application suite.

The primary selection criteria for our internal resources included

- Basic- to intermediate-level training on the Cognos suite of BI products. Training was coordinated by our IT department office prior to the start of the project
- Expert-level knowledge of all KFSH&RC computer systems that would be utilized in the data warehouse implementation
- Two to three years' experience in system development

ETL Development Team

The ETL subteam consisted of two FTEs from KFSH&RC and two from the vendor. The selection criteria we established for vendor personnel included

- Expert-level knowledge of the ETL process as it relates to data warehouse implementation
- Expert-level knowledge of the Informatica suite of products and of PL/SQL
- At least one member experienced in training to support the knowledge transfer of ETL processes with our staff

- Working knowledge of our Cerner-based Integrated Clinical Information System and Oracle Financial Application suite

We required the following of our internal ETL development staff:

- Basic- to intermediate-level training on the Informatica suite of ETL products and on PL/SQL. This training was scheduled prior to the project kickoff.
- Expert-level knowledge of all computer systems that feed the data warehouse
- Two to three years' experience in system development

Data Model/Database Development Team

As with the two other subteams, the Data Model/Database subteam consisted of two FTEs from our hospital and two from the vendor. The primary selection criteria for vendor-supplied personnel included

- Expert-level knowledge of logical and physical data-modeling processes relevant to data warehouse implementation
- Expert-level understanding of erwin data-modeling tools
- Expert-level knowledge of Oracle 10g databases
- At least one FTE with the expertise to train our staff on data modeling and database processes
- Paralleling the criteria established for the other subteams, we required our staff to undergo training in data modeling and Oracle 10g databases prior to the start of the project. This training was coordinated by the IT department. We also required subteam members to have working knowledge of our source system databases.

The above criteria were established to ensure our ability to deliver the data warehouse project on time and on budget. However, these criteria were established at the macro level. Given this gross capacity, our next task was to map the skill sets of the functional and technical development team members to the level of specific roles and responsibilities of each team and subteam. The following section details the roles and responsibilities assigned to each team and subteam.

Roles and Responsibilities

The development and maintenance of the data warehouse system required individual team members to assume the following roles and responsibilities:

- System requirements specification (SRS)
- Information analysis
- Design and data modeling
- Database build (DB build)
- ETL build
- Application (Cognos) build
- Unit/system integration testing
- User acceptance testing (UAT)
- Sign-off
- Support

As described previously, addressing each of these roles required a specific set of talents, perspectives, experiences, and skills. For example, those involved in SRS were primarily from the functional team. Requirements included a good understanding of hospital operation, considering the medical, clinical, financial, and logistical aspects. Staff assigned to information analysis and design and data-modeling tasks required a background in data architecture, good logical data-modeling skills, and a full understanding of the healthcare business.

Staff involved in the ETL and DB build phases required a full understanding of the source systems and database architectures, as well as solid programming skills. Development of the Cognos-based BI application and unit/system integration testing required staff with strong technical programming and problem solving skills, as well as an analytical mind-set. Cognos was selected because, based on our technical fact finding, it was the best available BI software at the time—a finding that was echoed by Gartner's assessments of 2003 and 2004. In addition, Cognos was strongly suggested by our data warehouse implementation vendor.

The functional team members involved in the acceptance phase required strong communication skills and, most importantly, the ability to market the deliverables to end users as useful decision-making tools.

As outlined above, the roles and responsibilities for data warehouse development was segregated into functional and technical areas, with a team of professionals assigned to each area as described in the following sections.

Table 5.4 Roles and Responsibilities of the Functional Team

Phase	Process	Output
SRS	KPI and report identification and definition; facilitate meeting with end users and technical team	SRS document
Information analysis	Clarification and feedback	Information analysis document
System integration testing	Assist in developing integration test cases with technical team; system and integration testing with technical team; define user access and security scheme	Deliverables ready for UAT
UAT	Develop acceptance test cases; acceptance test case finalization; acceptance testing; identify and record issues	Accepted deliveries
Acceptance	Approve deliverables; end-user training	Complete application
Maintenance	Provide first-line support to end users; initiate enhancement and maintenance tasks	Complete/close enhancement/ maintenance task

Functional Team Roles

As shown in Table 5.4, the functional team played a critical role in readiness assessment, business analysis, and developing a requirement specification document. As implied by the title, the role of the functional team was to provide a bridge between the end user community and the technical teams and to catalyze the transition from SRS to support.

Specific roles and responsibilities of the functional team at various phases of the project are summarized in Table 5.4 and outlined as follows:

- ■ SRS
    - Solicit and gather end user requirements.
    - Identify and define KPIs and analytical reports based on end user requirements.

- Facilitate meetings with end users and with OLAP and data-modeling technical team members.
- Produce a formal SRS document.
■ Information analysis
- Provide clarification on SRS to technical team if needed.
- Formulate strategies to overcome any process, system, or data gap identified in the information analysis document.
■ Application (Cognos)
- Review and provide feedback on OLAP application design.
■ System integration testing
- Develop integration test cases with the technical team.
- Conduct system and integration testing with the technical team.
- Define confidentiality, security, and user access needs with them.
■ UAT
- Develop UAT cases with end user.
- Finalize test cases.
- Conduct testing.
■ Acceptance
- Accept/approve deliverables (KPIs) in coordination with end users.
- Conduct end-user training.
■ Support
- Provide first-line support to end users.
- Initiate enhancement tasks based on end user feedback.

Technical Team Roles

The role of the technical team was more extensive than that of the functional team. As summarized in Table 5.5, the responsibilities of the technical team ranged from information analysis to the design of the data model to support.

The specific responsibilities of the technical team in various phases included

■ SRS
- Maintain active communication with the functional team.
■ Information analysis
- Meet end users for clarification on KPIs and reporting needs study.
- Source systems for the development of KPIs and reports.
- Identify process, system, or data gaps, if any.

Table 5.5 Roles and Responsibilities of the Technical Team

Phase	Process	Output
Information analysis	Study source system; identify gaps in source systems; update SRS document	Information analysis document
Design and data model finalization	Logical data modeling; physical data modeling; ETL design; OLAP design	Data model; ETL design document; OLAP design document
Database build	Design physical schema; build the database	Data warehouse (DW) and operational data store (ODS)
ETL build	Develop data extraction and mapping, transformation logic, loading scheme; develop ETL unit test cases; ETL unit testing	Data extraction, transformation, and loading scheme
OLAP build	Create packages, cubes, and reports; develop integration test cases; create user access and security structure; conduct system integration testing	Applications
System integration testing	Assemble ETL routines and OLAP deliverables; develop integration test cases; test user access and security structure; system integration testing	Deliverables ready for UAT
UAT	Assist functional team in acceptance testing; resolve issues	Accepted deliverables
Acceptance	Move deliverables to production; apply security structure in production	Complete application
Support	Technical support; maintenance and enhancement	Complete maintenance and enhancement task

- Provide feedback to the functional team for necessary updates in the SRS document.
- Produce information analysis documents.
■ Design and data model finalization
- Create a logical data model.
- Create a physical data model.
- Design ETL mappings.

- – Design OLAP deliverables in coordination with the functional team.
  - – Produce a logical/physical data model, ETL, and OLAP design documents.
- ◼ Database build
  - – Design physical schema.
  - – Build actual databases.
- ◼ ETL build
  - – Develop data extraction, transformation, and load mappings.
  - – Develop unit test cases for individual ETL mappings.
  - – Conduct an ETL unit test.
- ◼ Cognos (OLAP) build
  - – Create packages, cubes, and reports.
  - – Configure deliverables.
  - – Develop application unit test cases.
  - – Conduct a unit test.
  - – Configure the matrix manager, dashboards, and scorecards.
- ◼ System integration testing
  - – Assemble ETL mappings and OLAP deliverables.
  - – Develop an integration test case in coordination with the functional team.
  - – Test user access and security structure.
  - – Conduct system/integration testing in coordination with the functional team.
- ◼ UAT
  - – Participate in acceptance testing.
  - – Resolve issues arising from UAT.
- ◼ Acceptance
  - – Move OLAP deliverables into production.
  - – Provide user access and apply the security structure in production.
- ◼ Support
  - – Provide second- and third-line technical support.
  - – Maintain and enhance based on the functional team's input.

Life Cycle Variations

The relative involvement of the functional and technical teams varied considerably throughout the life of the project. As illustrated in Table 5.6, functional team members were involved predominantly in the SRS and system

Table 5.6 Life Cycle Variation in Roles and Responsibilities over Data Warehouse Life Cycle

Phase	End Users	Functional Team	Data Modelers	ETL Team	OLAP Team
SRS	X	X			
Information analysis		X	X	X	X
Design and data model finalization			X	X	X
Database build			X	X	
ETL build				X	
OLAP build					X
System integration testing		X		X	X
UAT	X	X		X	X
Acceptance	X	X			X
Support	X	X	X	X	X

and integration testing phases. Members of the technical team were involved in all but the initial SRS phase of the project.

In retrospect, we feel that the functional team should have been involved throughout the project. They should have worked with the OLAP team members in order to ensure smooth connectivity between end user expectation and OLAP deliverables. Similarly, the OLAP team members should have been involved with all parties—ETL, data modelers, DBA, functional team, and end users—for the entire duration of the project.

Development Team Hierarchies

The goals, objectives, and deliverables of the data warehouse project were shared by the vendor and KFSH&RC. However, the hierarchies within the development teams assembled by the vendor and KFSH&RC were significantly different.

Vendor

The vendor development team hierarchy was based on a strong matrix structure. This structure was combined with a project-oriented management system, illustrated in Table 5.7.

In this project-oriented structure, vendor team members were assigned on a project basis. Project managers exercised independence and complete authority over the deployed resources. The actual hierarchy established by the vendor is shown in Figure 5.1.

The vendor's project manager worked full time for the duration of the project. This project manager had full flexibility and control over scaling resources up or down as needed. He had full control from project initiation, planning, controlling, time management, and execution, up until project closure. The quality assurance coordinator was a part-time resource that was shared with other clients in the region.

Table 5.7　Project-Oriented Management Structure

Organization Structure	Functional	Matrix			Projective
		Weak Matrix	Balanced Matrix	Strong Matrix	
Project Characteristics					
Project manager's authority	Little or none	Limited	Low to moderate	Moderate to high	High to almost total
Resource availability	Little or none	Limited	Low to moderate	Moderate to high	High to almost total
Who controls the project budget	Functional manager	Functional manager	Mixed	Project manager	Project manager
Project manager's role	Part time	Part time	Full time	Full time	Full time
Project management administrative staff	Part time	Part time	Part time	Full time	Full time

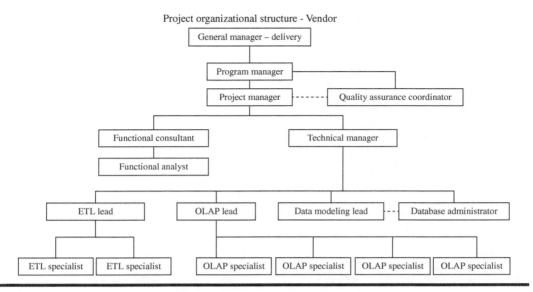

Project organizational structure - Vendor

Figure 5.1   Vendor development team hierarchy.

KFSH&RC

We followed a weak matrix structure in which the project manager's role was primarily coordinating and expediting. Furthermore, our staff maintained many of the characteristics of the functional units from which they were recruited. In this weak matrix structure, team members were not dedicated to a specific project. Similarly, the project manager spent most of his time coordinating the deployed resources. The hierarchy of resources we installed for the project at various stages is shown in Figure 5.2.

Resources were added at various stages of the project due to availability constraints.

Many of the resources were plugged into the project on a shared basis, where the project warranted fully dedicated resources, particularly in the functional, ETL, and data-modeling area. Furthermore, both the functional and technical project managers had responsibilities in other projects, as is typically the case with a weak matrix organizational structure. In addition, project managers had very little flexibility and control over the scaling up or down of available resources as needed in the various phases of the project. The weak matrix structure was a major impediment in the data warehouse project.

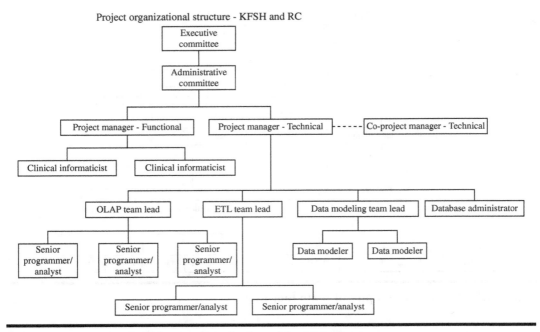

Figure 5.2 Hierarchy of resources deployed by KFSH&RC.

The project managers reported to a committee instead of a single executive. This reporting structure was a drawback as well. Although both the Executive and Administrative Committees consisted of senior and executive management with superb decision-making skills and access to organization-wide audiences, the committees also added considerable overheads. Obtaining a consensus from these committees, particularly from the Administrative Committee, was extremely challenging. Despite their shortcomings, the committees facilitated the definition of formulae as well as exclusion and inclusion criterion for many of the analytical reports and KPIs.

Lessons Learned

- Teams should be composed of vendor- and internally supplied personnel.
- Team members should be carefully selected with the appropriate skill sets.
- Regular interaction among all members of the various teams is essential.
- The functional team should keep end users informed of development progress.

- The active involvement of the functional team throughout the project is critical.
- OLAP team members need to keep all parties—ETL, data modelers, DBA, functional team, and end users—in the loop for the entire duration of the project.
- Implementation would have been more effective if the appropriate resources were available throughout the duration of the project, instead of pulled from other projects on an ad hoc basis.
- Exercising the weak matrix structure in project setting should be avoided by all means.
- Obtaining the necessary leverage in a large and complex organization such as ours was certainly a challenge, but we overcame it through the involvement of the Executive and Administrative Committees.
- Careful selection and even representation of members of the Executive and Administrative Committees was extremely important.
- The smooth and timely flow of information between the Executive Committee, the Administrative Committee, and the functional and technical teams was critical for the successful implementation of the data warehouse project.

Chapter 6

Planning

Enam UL Hoque

Contents

Developing a data warehouse is challenging compared with typical application development because it is a new discipline without well-established strategies and techniques. Many data warehouse initiatives fail due to the complexities of the development processes—especially poor planning. This chapter provides an overview of our planning process.

Perspective

During the past decade, various methods have been applied to the process of data warehouse development. These approaches can be grouped into three basic methods: goal driven, user driven, and data driven. The aims of all three approaches are the same: to analyze and improve business processes. We chose a combination of the goal- and user-driven approaches.

Goals

In developing a data warehouse, it is important to note that value comes not from the technology itself but from the use of information transformed out of the data in the warehouse. Use, in turn, requires substantial organizational change as well as the full support, commitment, and involvement of top management. With these caveats in mind, during the planning stage we established several high-level goals—in effect, a requirement specification—and included these goals in our request for proposal (RFP). We stipulated that the data warehouse should provide

- An improved method of storing and retrieving data, thereby enabling our users to make informed decisions
- The ability for our management to access, analyze, and explore information and achieve improved, informed, and fact-based decision making
- Operational efficiencies from the reduction in the time and effort required to request, extract, and analyze data
- Readily available historical information for trend analysis
- Greater access to superior and timely information so that it can more effectively meet the needs of patients, governments, employees, and suppliers
- Information that's presented in a sophisticated, graphical way that supports the intuitive exploration of the data by senior management
- Easy implementation so that the transfer of knowledge and skills from the vendor to our staff is seamless

Process

Our development process consisted of three phases, as illustrated in Figure 6.1. Each process within a phase was driven by a set of goals that included deliverables from the vendor. The deliverable for the planning phase was the system requirements specification (SRS) document. The primary deliverables for the design phase included extraction, transformation, and loading (ETL) and online analytical processing (OLAP) design. The implementation phase consisted of creating the ETL and OLAP builds and

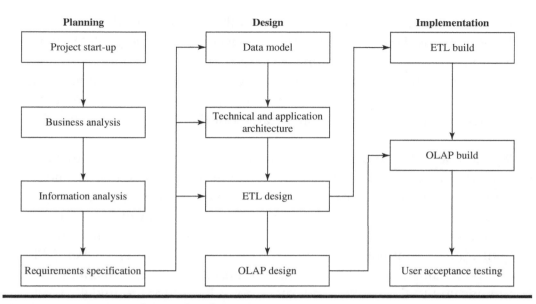

Figure 6.1   Data warehouse development process.

promoting user acceptance. Each phase required significant coordination between our staff and the vendor.

The major activities performed during the planning phase were project start-up, business analysis, information analysis, and the development of a requirement specification document. These activities are described in more detail below.

Project Start-Up

During project start-up, members of our staff, the vendor, and other major stakeholders were oriented to the scope, boundaries, time lines, and deliverables of the project. Data warehouse concepts were also presented and reviewed by the vendor and our staff. Topics covered included

- Overview of data warehouses and business intelligence
- Data warehouse architecture
- Data modeling
- Data warehouse databases
- Data quality and ETL
- Metadata
- Data warehouse development process model

During the initial meeting, we reviewed the project with the vendor and discussed decision support needs in the context of the goals defined in our RFP. Following this meeting, management from every department participating in the project was interviewed. Our objectives were to examine the current performance measures and reports, explore their relevance to the decision-making process, and frame out the deliverables of the data warehouse.

Within a few days of the initial meeting, we developed a prioritized list of key performance indicators (KPIs) that were relevant from departmental and organizational perspectives. We identified the variables, equations, data sources, technical limitations, and accuracy of the available data for the ranked KPIs and presented that information to the Data Warehouse Administrative Committee, who had the final say in whether a given KPI was to be included in the first iteration of implementation. This final list was communicated to the vendor. Indicators not selected for the initial round of implementation were set aside for potential inclusion at a later date.

Business Analysis

Business analysis, one of the most important activities within the planning stage, involves gathering the functional and informational requirements for analytical reporting. Through interviews, we identified three key areas for business analysis: clinical departments, nonclinical departments, and the corporate office.

We interviewed the heads and staff of Emergency Medicine, Cardiology, Intensive Care Units (MSICU, PICU, and NICU), Oncology, Operating Room, Nursing, Radiology, Pharmacy, and Pathology. We also interviewed the heads and staff of nonclinical departments, including Eligibility, Appointments, Medical Records, Human Resources, Payroll, Finance, and Logistics. Our staff clearly defined the objectives and desired outcomes prior to each interview.

As part of business analysis, we identified the core decision-making and reporting needs in terms of the ranked list of KPIs. In this context, KPIs are the core measures that we rely on to gauge the performance of the various departments and areas of our organization. Specifically, we were looking at how an indicator has performed in the past and how it is currently doing. Examples of KPIs we identified as critical include average length of stay, mortality, bed utilization, bed turnover rate, and medication error rate.

We established a task force to review and validate all KPIs with the end user departments. As a part of the validation process, the task force challenged and questioned the nature and appropriateness of the KPI. If it deemed that the KPI would not benefit the end user or the organization, the task force was empowered to drop the KPI. Similarly, if the task force felt that a departmental KPI would be of value to one or more departments, it could consider applying the KPI at the corporate level.

The vendor's quality assurance team reviewed the KPIs. The final KPI definition, in the form of a functional document, was submitted to the Data Warehousing Committee for approval. Sign-off of these functional documents was a major milestone established by our contract with the vendor. To highlight the magnitude of the business analysis phase, 325 KPIs were identified at the end of the initial round of requirement gatherings. These KPIs were analyzed and consolidated into 196 KPIs that were defined using the template shown in Appendix II.

Information Analysis

Information analysis was performed for every KPI defined during the business analysis stage. The primary objectives of information analysis were to

- Study relevant source systems with a view to mapping business requirements to available source systems
- Develop report layouts, including data elements, frequency of reporting, and availability of source data, for the actual development and implementation
- Identify the dimensions, required attributes, hierarchies, measures, filter conditions, and adjustments for KPIs
- Identify gaps in the availability of the source system, data elements, and data
- Recommend the remediation of identified gaps

Information analysis involved an in-depth study of the source systems for the required data. This required a mapping of data sources to business requirements to help identify the candidate source systems that would provide the data necessary to fulfill the business requirements. Source systems were also analyzed to assess the quality and availability of stored data. Information analysis includes

- Mapping KPI data elements to source system attributes
- Relationship of the entities involved in order to map all departmental KPIs
- Details of the aggregated data elements (dimensions and hierarchies)
- Granular-level data element
- Measures and derived measures and any other calculated parameters
- Filter conditions required to map the exact data content
- Attributes and the associated attributes required for a KPI
- Analysis of the source entities, entity relationships, and data elements of sources
- Mapping of the KPI requirements to source data elements
- Documentation of data dimensions, attributes, hierarchies (including granularity), measures, inclusion and exclusion populations, adjustment formulas, and null conditions
- Validation of the data elements by the functional team
- Scheduling frequency of the reports

Report Layout

Finalizing the report layout involved validating the data elements identified by the end user departments, as defined in the information analysis document. Validation of the final report layout was performed by the functional consultant in conjunction with end users. This validation was included in the information analysis document.

Gap Analysis

A gap analysis was performed using the data elements and business facts gathered for the development of the information analysis document. The goal of the gap analysis was to identify the differences between the information that will be required and the current and planned capabilities of the data warehouse.

Two types of gaps emerged during the analysis of each KPI: gaps in process and gaps in data. Process gaps reflected the lack of a mechanism to capture the required data from the source system. Data gaps reflected our inability to extract data from a system. A gap analysis document was prepared and submitted by the vendor as part of their deliverables and we reviewed, validated, and signed off on it.

User Acceptance Criteria

Establishing user acceptance criteria, an important aspect of the planning phase, involved subjective and objective assessments. System functionality was tested on a departmental basis, relative to the requirements contained in the SRS documents. An overarching requirement was that the presentation layer, using the Cognos Business Intelligence tools, should be accurate with respect to source systems and that performance should meet the benchmark criteria established by the Cognos Corporation. Performance criteria also reflected the nature of reports (e.g., simple, medium, or complex) and our final hardware configuration.

In working with the vendor, we established the following ground rules regarding acceptance criteria:

■ We were to consolidate all problems in any deliverable made by the vendor and report the problem within two weeks of receipt of the deliverable. Problems included bugs, errors, and deviations from the functionality specified in the SRS document and did not include scope enhancements. Scope enhancements were handled separately in an established change management procedure.
■ The vendor was to rectify any problems identified by our team and resubmit the deliverable. We were given one week to note any problems with the fixes within a release and one week to resubmit. The vendor was liable to fix only those problems pertaining to the fixes done in the specified release and not the problems reported in other areas of the deliverable.
■ If we or the vendor raised issues outside of the fixes done in the specified release, the vendor was to fix them on a cost recovery basis.

System Requirements Specification

Review, validation, and quality assessment were critical in finalizing the SRS. Not only did data validation and quality checking form the basis for the creation of the gap analysis document, but a quality assessment process was also used to verify the data were correct and complete. Of the original 196 KPIs we defined, 43 had a gap in either data or process and 21 were dropped because of administrative reasons. Validation and revision were conducted jointly by our team and by the vendor. An example of the information analysis component of the SRS, based on average length of stay, is provided in Appendix III.

Review, validation, and quality assessment were conducted at four levels. The Level 1 review consisted of document validation by the vendor. The vendor created queries for analyzing the source application and a gap analysis was performed on the results. Level 2 reviews, performed by our functional team, consisted of validating the report layouts, data elements, and decision making linked to a given KPI. The Level 3 review was primarily a quality assessment of the information analysis document. The review was performed by the vendor's technical project lead and then by our technical project manager. During the Level 4 review, our technical team reviewed and validated the information analysis document for source system mapping, for the report layout, and for the gap analysis. Modifications suggested during the review process were sent to the original document author and the updated documents were recirculated.

Creating the SRS required documenting the planning phase processes discussed in earlier sections. As a review, developing the SRS document involved the following:

- Preparing for assembling business requirements
- Defining business requirements
- Identifying and defining the business KPIs
- Analyzing and mapping business requirements to source systems
- Performing information analysis on the KPIs
- Identifying gaps discovered during information analysis
- Recommending a solution to fill the gaps
- Reviewing, validating, and assessing quality
- Defining user acceptance criteria
- Preparing the consolidated SRS document

The complete SRS document was submitted by the vendor for our review and sign-off along three metrics: data availability to the warehouse; accuracy, including the identification of the single source of truthful data when there were multiple sources; and quality in the transformation and cleanup of data destined for the data warehouse.

Lessons Learned

■ Business analysis resulted in a marked reduction of the KPIs actually developed.
■ Planning is a multistep process that requires full vendor and client participation.
■ High-level goals and development processes should be clearly defined as part of the planning.
■ High-level goals or requirements specification should be shared with prospective vendors in the RFP.
■ User acceptance criteria should be clearly defined.
■ Gap analysis should be conducted thoroughly and reviewed carefully.
■ SRS documentation should include recommended solutions to fill the gaps.

Chapter 7

Design

Fadwa Saad AlBawardi and Enam UL Hoque

Contents

This chapter, written by the project leader and the technical manager of the data warehouse project, provides an overview of our technical design. It includes a discussion of the data model; the logical and physical architecture; the underlying data model; the extraction, transformation, and loading (ETL) process; provision for backup and recovery; and reporting.

Creating a data warehouse is a complex process that demands careful management, insightful leadership, adequate resources, and, above all, good technical design. Our data warehouse design process began with data modeling, including the definition of metadata. Major design decisions associated with developing our data model included establishing naming standards, operating parameters, dimensions, and keys, as well as the overall configuration. In addition, data standardization is essential during the design process. Standardization is the process of transforming data from disparate systems and sources into a consistent format. Standardizing data is a critical step in a data quality process because it makes it easier to identify issues, errors, and outliers within data sets. It also makes data easier to audit, govern, and analyze, and insures data reliability. The process and resulting data model parameters are described in this chapter.

Data Model

Our data model is based on the source systems and data element mapping as defined in the system requirements specification (SRS) document, following the dimensional data-modeling approach. This technique allowed us the flexibility to analyze and access available data from the various source systems. Mapping, one of the essential steps in this technique, is a process wherein business requirements are translated into the technical allocation of tables/fields within the source system databases and the data warehouse database. We also used an enterprise-wide data model design for an integrated view of hospital business areas. Integration was achieved through conformed dimensions—an amalgamation and distillation of data from several sources. For example, we used the conformed dimension of *location*, providing us with a single master list of location-defined beds in terms of room, nursing unit, building, and region/facility.

The logical and physical data models, designed using the AllFusion ERwin Data Modeler from Computer Associates International, rely on subject areas with *dimension* and *fact* tables represented in both star and snowflake schema. A fact is an event or transaction that is updated, counted, or measured, such as patient admission or patient discharge. A dimension contains related reference information about the fact, such as patient admission/discharge dates, diagnosis, or medications. A star schema is diagramed by surrounding each fact with its associated dimensions. The resulting diagram resembles a star. Features of the star schema include the ability to process large, complex, ad hoc, and data-intensive queries, with little concern for concurrency, locking, and insert/update/delete performance. Each fact table has a composite key that is joined to denormalized, single-level dimension tables, and each table has a single primary key. Numerical measures are stored in the fact tables, and attributes about facts are stored in dimension tables. An example of a star schema is shown in Figure 7.1.

The snowflake schema, a variation of the star schema, relies on a flat, single-table dimension that is decomposed into a multilevel tree structure. In the snowflake schema, dimensions are normalized into multiple related tables, whereas the star schema's dimensions are denormalized with each dimension represented by a single table. Characteristics of the snowflake schema include good performance when the queries involve aggregation, the use of a single key for each level of the dimension's hierarchy, and the normalization of tables by decomposing at the attribute level. Unfortunately, a snowflake schema requires complicated maintenance, and the size and number of tables increase along with their metadata (in cases where there are updated requirements to involve new information, the metadata scope would have to change accordingly). An example of a snowflake schema is shown in Figure 7.2.

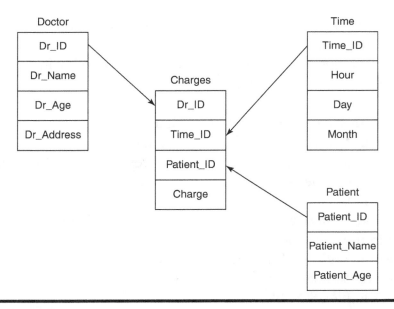

Figure 7.1 Star schema.

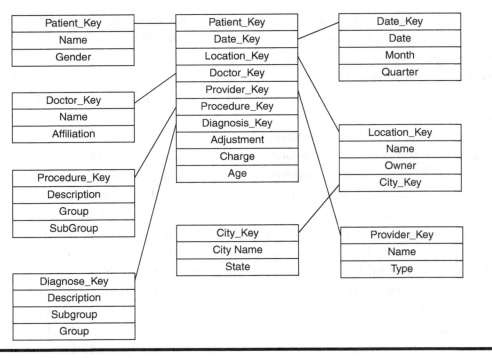

Figure 7.2 Snowflake schema.

Design Process

A prerequisite to beginning the design process was to thoroughly understand the business processes and available data sources within our organization. Once this milestone was achieved, we used the following data model design process:

- Choose the subject areas to be modeled.
- Identify and design the conformed dimensions.
- Define the dimension granularity (the lowest level of information to be stored in the dimension tables).
- Design the facts.
- Determine the fact granularity (the lowest level of information to be stored in the fact tables).
- Transform conceptual design to physical design.
  - Naming standards and conventions.
    - Data files/SQL files
    - Database
    - Application

    – Character case.
    – Apply design considerations for database parameters.
    – Define fact and dimension tables as the physical data model.

Although the process is presented linearly, the design of our data model was actually an iterative process. The first step in the design process was to choose the subject areas to be modeled. Areas that we have initially selected included Employee, Operating Room, Encounter, Appointments, and Eligibility. For each of these areas, we developed an information requirement specification document that contained specifics about the source tables/fields and the target tables/fields. In later stages of the project, we added more subject areas, including Lab, Medical Imaging/Radiology, Pharmacy, and Finance.

Conformed dimensions are consistent sets of data attributes, where data replication is avoided and the data warehouse is enabled to function as an integrated whole. In identifying and designing conformed dimensions, we identified data model dimensions, their attributes, and fields. For example, when the conformed dimension *location* is applied to patients, it includes region/facility, building, nursing unit, room, and bed. When it is applied to employees, however, it includes region/facility, department, division, section, and unit. Conformed dimensions enable the data warehouse to function as an integrated whole. An associated task was defining the granularity of each conformed dimension. For example, in the case of location, granularity was to the level of individual patients and employees. In designing the facts, we identified data model facts, their attributes, and fields. Fact tables contain the transactional data that are updated daily, weekly, monthly, quarterly, or annually.

Transforming the conceptual design to a physical design involved adhering to a fixed naming convention, a definitive parameter list, and an underlying dimensional data-modeling approach. For example, we used a standard naming convention for data files/SQL files, database schema objects, and applications.

We also sized several key database parameters to ensure acceptable loading and overall system response times. For example, we have a DB_FILES database parameter that specifies the maximum number of database files that can be opened for a database. Similarly, MAX_ENABLED_ROLES specifies the maximum number of database roles that users can enable, including roles contained within other roles. (See Appendix IV for a list of other parameters.)

The key challenges we faced during the data model design process were related to the limited availability of data, the cleansing of some existing data, and the timing of the planned data updates. Specifically, data for some of the key source systems, such as Mainframe DB2, Btrieve, and Lotus Domino, were not available in the desired format. The data model for these areas was developed during the information analysis. When data gaps were identified, we secured agreements with the end users to enter data manually. Similarly, we made provision to alter the data model to reflect changes in the source systems, thereby insuring consistency within the data warehouse. We identified data that had to be cleaned at the source level, as well as data that needed to be cleaned during the ETL cycle. In addition, we verified that fact tables were updated during each ETL cycle to ensure data accuracy and consistency with respect to source systems.

Architecture

This section outlines the design of the logical and physical architectures of our data warehouse. The logical architecture defines the integration of logical components, whereas the physical architecture describes hardware configuration, operating system, and file system.

Logical Architecture

The logical architecture of our data warehouse, shown in Figure 7.3, incorporates both data and applications. We have several source applications, including Cerner ICIS, Q-matic, and Oracle Financials, as well as home-grown in-house applications on our mainframe. The source applications use a variety of database and file formats, including Microsoft Access and flat files. We use an Informatica server, an Oracle 10g repository, and an Oracle 10g staging area to perform the ETL operations from the applications and other data sources.

We have an operational data store (ODS) and enterprise data warehouse, both implemented in Oracle 10g. The ODS enables near real-time reporting of key performance indicators (KPIs). The enterprise data warehouse provides a buffer between the source systems and the query applications. This design protects the source systems from the impact of the intense, periodic ETL activity. The performance of the source systems may be heavily impacted if the ETL activity is used directly during the utilization time. Separate databases, implemented in Oracle 9i, are used for Cognos Report Net and Cognos Metrics Manager repositories.

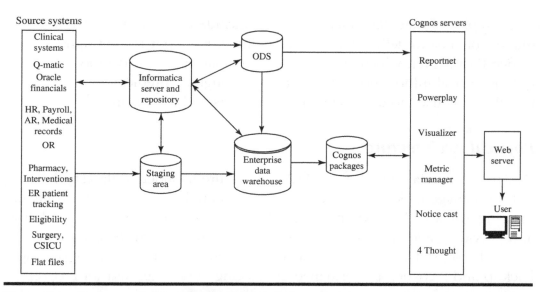

Figure 7.3 Data warehouse logical architecture.

We also employ a web server that feeds PC workstations with data from an array of Cognos tools, including ReportNet, PowerPlay, Visualizer, Metrics Manager, Notice Cast, and 4Thought. Cognos ReportNet is a report publishing and management product that includes a server, an ad hoc reporting tool, a report development tool, a data modeling and management tool, and a web portal. With the exception of the data management tool, all the ReportNet components are delivered via zero-footprint web browsers and are managed by a separate ReportNet server.

Cognos PowerPlay enables us to report from both the client platform and over the web. Online analytical processing (OLAP) data sources or *cubes* are created by the *transformer*. A cube is a multidimensional data source that contains data and measures (calculations of this data). It is organized into dimensions and added to PowerPlay Enterprise Server or the Cognos portal. PowerPlay Enterprise Server acts as the OLAP application server for PowerPlay for Windows and PowerPlay Web, providing cube access to users. With PowerPlay Enterprise Server, we can access not only Cognos's proprietary PowerCubes and our Analysis Services Cubes but also numerous other third-party cubes.

A limitation of the Cognos toolset is that it evolved during the project, with some tools becoming obsolete with new versions of the software. Cognos Business Intelligence and Cognos Insight tools are used in the current version of our data warehouse.

Examples of outdated Cognos toolsets include Cognos Visualizer, a tool that enabled us to deliver interactive, multimetric graphics; the Cognos Notice Cast Server, which enabled us to automatically alert decision makers to time-critical information; and Cognos 4Thought, a predictive modeling tool that was used to automate what-if analysis and forecasting.

Physical Architecture

Design issues related to the physical architecture included scalability, how to best manage table sizing and partitioning, handling capacity and volume, insuring availability, providing acceptable performance, maintaining stability, and providing adequate security and data governance. Our goal was to create a reliable, stable system capable of efficiently and effectively supporting backup and recovery, performance monitoring, reporting, disaster recovery, version control, and configuration management.

The hardware and software configurations of the development and production servers are listed in Appendix V. Highlights of the physical architecture design include the following:

- The ODS, which was implemented in Oracle 10g, was designed to generate near real-time KPIs.
- Separate staging/temporary areas were created to form a logical and physical separation between the source systems and the data warehouse database. This minimized the impact of the intense periodic ETL activity on source and data warehouse databases. Staging areas were implemented separately in Oracle 10g.
- A separate database was created for the data warehouse dimensional model.
- Staging Oracle 10g had a separate schema for the Informatica repository.
- Separate databases were created for the Cognos Report Net and Cognos Metrics Manager repositories. Both repositories were implemented in the same Oracle 9i instance.
- Informatica PowerExchange was used to extract data from Mainframe VSAM and the DB2 database.
- Informatica PowerCenter was used to extract data from relational databases and flat files.
- IBM Storage Solution was used to store database files and Cognos Cube files.

- All machines were connected to the external storage with a backup mechanism to ensure data recovery in case of failure.
- RAID5 was used to ensure recovery in case of media failure.
- The Informatica repository was used to store technical metadata such as source system connections, source and target table structures, and mappings and transformations.
- Cognos Framework Manager and Metrics Manager repositories were used to store business metadata such as measures, dimensions, hierarchy, packages, reports, and scorecards.
- Single-sign-on was implemented across all products/components of Cognos.

We did not incorporate redundancy at the component level. However, our design did support scaling with additional software and hardware components.

Extraction, Transformation, and Loading

Efficient, accurate, and complete ETL operations are essential for the proper operation of a data warehouse. During extraction, the data from the source systems are transferred to a staging area. The transformation process involves cleaning and transforming the data. In the loading process, data from the staging area are loaded into the data warehouse databases. The extraction process starts at midnight daily, when there is minimum utilization of the source systems, and finishes within a few hours, before normal working hours.

Extraction

As illustrated in Figure 7.4, during the extraction phase of our ETL operations, data from our Cerner, Mainframe, Oracle Financials, SQL Server, Btrieve, Microsoft Access, Q-matics, DB2 UDB, Lotus Domino, and dBase source systems are transferred to the staging area en route to the ODS and data warehouse.

Our extraction operations are of two types: full and incremental. Full extraction includes the full Informatica mappings from the source systems. Full extraction usually takes place with small databases that have frequent record changes. Incremental extraction takes care of extracting

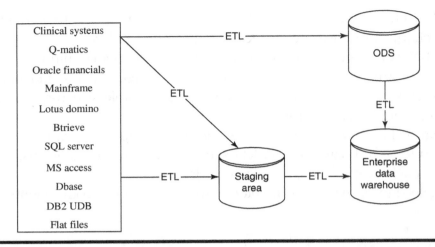

Figure 7.4 ETL process.

only newly added/changed daily transactional data from the source system on an incremental basis. As illustrated in Figure 7.4, mappings include source to staging area, staging area to data warehouse, and source to ODS.

One of the important functions of the staging area is to provide an environment supportive of storing transactional data in a way that allows simple and fast transformation, and the loading of data into the OLAP system. In addition to forming a logical and physical separation between the source systems and the data warehouse database, the staging area database reduces the effect of the concentrated periodic ETL activity on source and data warehouse databases. Data staging buffers the source systems from the demands of the data warehouse.

The ODS serves a role similar to that of the staging area, with the exception that the ODS is designed to integrate near real-time operational information from different systems in support of near real-time reporting. The ODS is a subject-oriented, integrated database implemented in Oracle 10g. Details of the ETL process and its relationship to the staging area and ODS are illustrated in Figure 7.5.

Because full extraction encompasses all the data available on the source systems, there is no need to keep track of changes to the data source since the last extraction. Incremental extraction, in contrast, only considers data that have changed since the last extraction (if any). Data that have been altered since the last incremental extraction are identified by a timestamp.

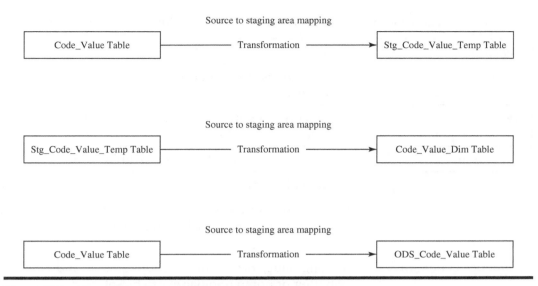

Figure 7.5   Examples of extraction mappings.

Transformation

Transformation is an important feature and an essential stage in the ETL process. Transformations such as filtering, sorting, lookup, and calculations are required to ensure standardization, high quality, accuracy, consistency, a lack of data conflicts, and the compatibility of data sources accumulated from a variety of systems. We rely on Informatica to transform data in the staging area. Additional transformations are used when moving data from the staging area to the data warehouse database. Table 7.1 lists the transforms we use on data destined for the data warehouse.

Loading

ETL are involved at multiple points in the data warehouse. There are two forms of loading: initial full loading and daily incremental loading. The initial, full load involves loading old archival data that resides in online transaction processing (OLTP) into the data warehouse. This type of load is performed only once. After data from the sources have been extracted, transformed, and combined, the loading operation consists of inserting records into the various data warehouse database dimension and fact tables.

Daily incremental loading is an ongoing refresh process used to selectively load data from the sources to the staging area. These incremental

Table 7.1 Transformations Used on Data Destined for the Data Warehouse

Transformation	*Usage*
Source qualifier	Used to define the reader process or the selection for relational sources.
Lookup	To look up tables in the source, target, or other database.
Expression	There are more than 80 functions within PowerCenter.
Filter	Used to filter data.
Normalizer	Used to normalize source data. PowerCenter does this automatically. The normalizer is also used to pivot data.
Sequence generator	Starting value, increment value, upper limit, and whether or not to reinitialize can be set.
Joiner	Used for heterogeneous joins within a mapping (e.g., a flat file with an Oracle table).
Update strategy	Used to finely control on a row-by-row basis whether we want the row to be inserted, updated, deleted, or rejected, based on some logical condition we have derived in the mapping process.
Sorter	Used to sort the data in ascending or descending order, generally used before the aggregation of data.
Aggregator	Used with functions that require the sorting of a group.
Router	Used for branching. Tests data for one or more conditions and provides the user with the option to route rows of data that do not meet any of the conditions to a default output group.
Rank	Used with a specific data mart, such as Top Performers. Can load the top 5 products and the top 100 customers—or the bottom 5 products.
Stored procedure	PowerCenter eliminated the need for coding

data are identified by timestamps maintained by the source system. As with initial loading, once the data from the data sources have been extracted, transformed, and combined, the loading operation consists of inserting records into the various data warehouse database dimension and fact tables.

Backup and Recovery

Data backup and provision for rapid, errorless recovery are essential to guarantee the integrity of the data warehouse. As such, our technical design features two types of backups. The first type is physical backup, which involves copying and recovering physical database files. The second type of backup is logical, dealing with data exported using SQL commands and stored in binary files. Logical backups are insurance against user error, such as inadvertently dropping a table or column.

Table 7.2 summarizes our backup design for the operating system, staging area, ODS, and data warehouse database. The frequency of the backup varies as needed from daily, weekly, fortnightly, monthly, or quarterly, and the backup can be full or incremental. Operating system backups are handled by the system administrator and the remaining backups are assigned to DBA IT support.

Our database backup process is designed to guard against the following failures:

- *Instance*: A problem that prevents an Oracle instance from continuing to function. When an instance fails, Oracle does not write the data in the buffers to disc.
- *Process*: A failure in a user process that is accessing Oracle. If the user process fails while modifying the database, Oracle background processes undo the effects of uncommitted transactions.
- *Statement*: A logical failure in the handling statement in an Oracle program. When statement failure occurs, Oracle automatically undoes any effects of the statement and returns control to the user.
- *Media*: A physical problem with the media during an Oracle write or read operation.
- *Disk*: A problem with the disk drives can affect a variety of files, including data files, redo log files, and control files.
- *Application*: An internal application error results in a loss of data.
- *User error*: A user mistake results in a loss of data.

We rely on Oracle Recovery Manager (RMAN), an Enterprise Manager–based command line tool, for backup and restore operations. Restoring a physical backup involves recreating it and making it available to the Oracle server. To recover a restored backup, the data are updated using *redo* records from the transaction log. The transaction log records all changes made to the database after creating a backup. Table 7.3 summarizes our data recovery policy and responsibility.

Table 7.2   Data Warehouse Backup Strategy

Backup	Backup Policy				Remarks
	Frequency	*Mode*	*Medium*	*Responsibility*	
Operating system	Daily	Full	Tape	System administrator	Includes operating system, file systems, and Oracle file systems.
Staging area	Daily	Full	Tape	DBA IT support	Data retention should not be more than a week.
Staging area	Weekly	Full	Tape	DBA IT support	
Staging area	Daily	Incremental	Tape	DBA IT support	Required if staging retention is more than a day.
ODS	Weekly	Full	Tape	DBA IT support	
ODS	Daily	Full	Tape	DBA IT support	ODS retention is 1 day.
Data warehouse DB	Biweekly	Full	Tape	DBA IT support	
Data warehouse DB	Daily	Incremental	Tape	DBA IT support	
Data warehouse DB	Monthly	Cold	Tape	DBA IT support	
Data warehouse DB	Monthly	Full	Tape	DBA IT support	For specific tables.
Data warehouse DB	Quarterly	Cold	Tape	DBA IT support	
Data warehouse DB	Quarterly	Full	Tape	DBA IT support	For specific tables.

Table 7.3 Data Recovery Policy and Responsibility

Failure	Recovery Policy	Responsibility	Remarks
Operating system	Recovery of operating system.	System administrator	
Oracle database software	Recovery of Oracle database software from OS backups.	System administrator/DBA IT support	
User statement	Oracle will automatically undo an effect and return control to user.	Oracle	No user intervention required
Oracle user process	Oracle background process will automatically undo the effects of uncommitted transactions	Oracle	No user intervention required
Oracle instance	Restart the instance after analyzing the failure cause	DBA IT support	Recovery time depends on the type of instance failure
Hardware	Recovery from offline backups	DB IT support	Recovery time depends on offline backup tape retention policy

Reporting

Our reporting design is based on the Cognos web-enabled toolset, which supports dynamic querying and reporting. The suite of reporting tools includes Cognos ReportNet for dynamic reports and Cognos Cubes for analytical reports. As mentioned earlier, we also use Metrics Manager score-cards and Visualizer dashboards for analyzing and reporting KPIs together with benchmarking. The reporting architecture design is summarized in Figure 7.6.

We offer our hospital staff, executive managers, and administrators several types of reports, which fit the level of utilization capability of each key user—mainly analytical reports, detailed reports, dashboards, and

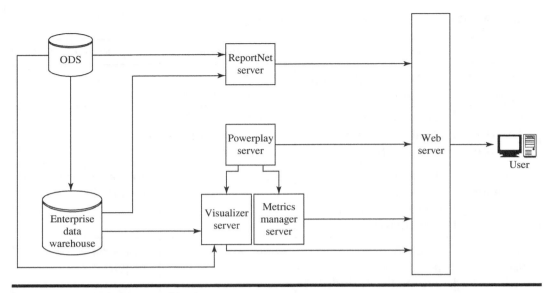

Figure 7.6   Reporting architecture.

scorecards. Analytical reports have drill-through and drill-down capabilities that represent the KPI measures according to any particular choice of dimensions. Detailed reports are fixed reports that show columns with details of any specific measure. Dashboards present the KPIs with intuitive, graphical gauges, charts, and tables within a web browser. Dashboards are useful when there is a need to present a large number of variables in a single, integrated view. Another advantage of dashboards is the ability to roll up details into high-level summaries. Figures 7.7 and 7.8 show actual dashboards developed for our institution, related to patient discharges and mortality rates. We have created hundreds of dashboards for our key departments/users.

In addition, near real-time dashboards were created to display indicators that are important to track by the hour, every day. For example, the average waiting time of patients in the Pharmacy, Phlebotomy, and Radiology departments are displayed in near real-time dashboards, with about 1 h difference. These dashboards highlight excessive patient waiting times. The average waiting time of patients is one of the most important measures that reflect the level of patient care. The less the waiting time, the better the patient care.

A scorecard, such as the one in Figure 7.9, is a table of KPIs arranged to provide a unique view of the healthcare organization with the

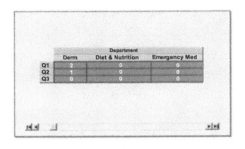 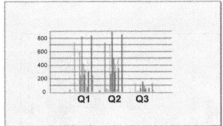

 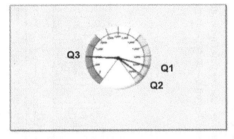

Figure 7.7   Discharges dashboard.

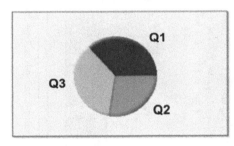 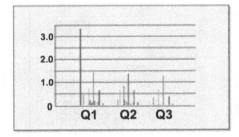

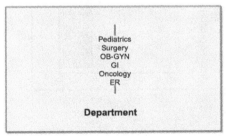 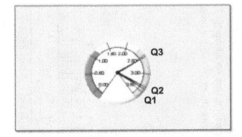

Figure 7.8   Mortality rate dashboard.

benchmarking feature. In particular, when the scorecard combines multiple perspectives—for example, medical care, quality of care, employees, education and research, financials, customers, internal processes, and employee learning and growth—into a single table in a balanced fashion, it becomes a tool for assessing management strategy. These mixed-perspective scorecards

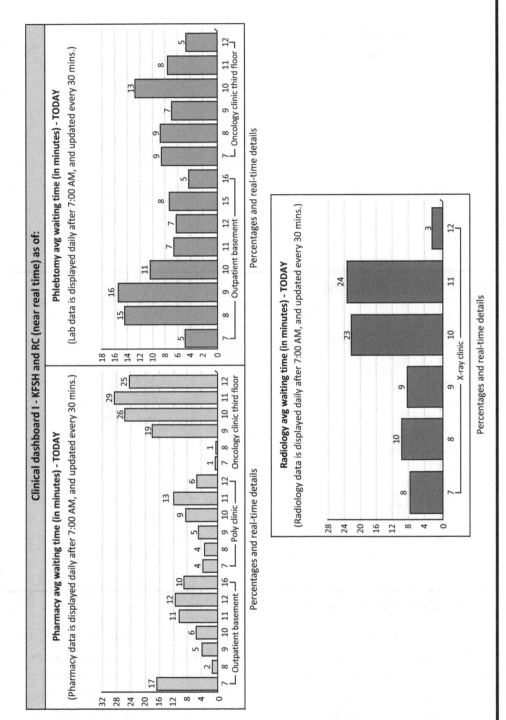

Figure 7.9 Scorecards.

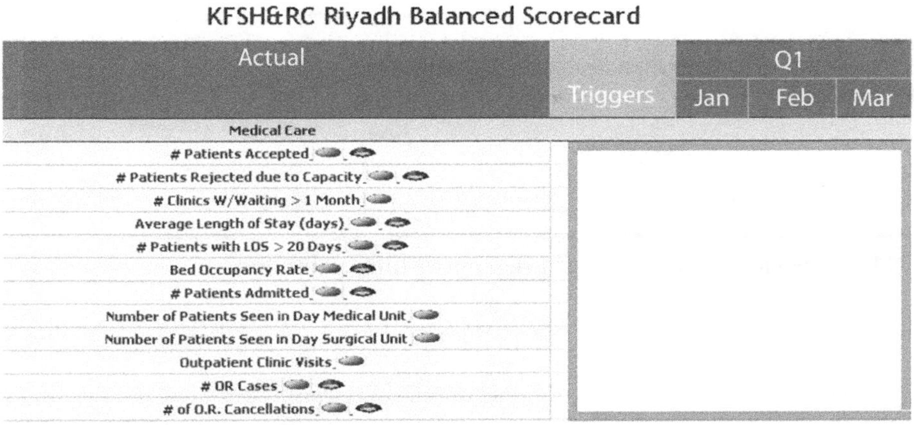

KFSH&RC Riyadh Balanced Scorecard

Figure 7.10   Balanced scorecard.

are referred to as *balanced* when the same number of KPIs is used to represent each of the multiple perspectives.

A balanced scorecard, automated using the business intelligence cycle, is shown in Figure 7.10. It is an annual report at an organizational level that gets automatically updated every month—with the monthly/quarterly figure related to the specific indicators in the scorecard. The trigger is the benchmark value, which controls how the performance of each indicator is measured—good or bad—in the various perspectives. Developing the automated balanced scorecard was one of the most important milestones we achieved during the data warehousing project.

In addition to the higher-level balanced scorecard, several drill-down nursing, operational, and departmental scorecards were also created.

Reports are generated as a function of user needs—daily, weekly, monthly, or annually. Reports can be automatically sent to users with the appropriate security permissions via email, or the reports can be archived to a server in a variety of formats, including PDF and Excel. Access to reports can be defined down to the data's lower-most granular level. Screens from the various reports can be used within PowerPoint presentations, for demo or reporting purposes.

The importance of creating reports for analysis and performance comparison can be illustrated in the design of the physician workload profile, which summarizes the performance/productivity measures of each physician per month, quarter, or year. The performance/productivity measures report can also be enhanced to show related figures per day or week, if

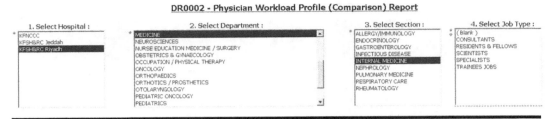

Figure 7.11   Physician workload profile report filter selection.

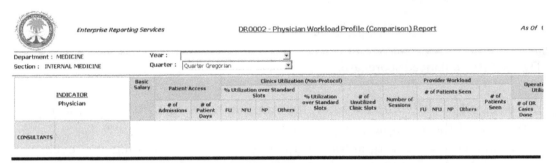

Figure 7.12   Physician workload profile report.

needed. As shown in Figure 7.11, executives can choose to select to view physician workload by the hospital, department, section, and job type of any physicians.

Figure 7.12 shows how the resulting report will display the various performance/productivity measures for the selected physicians so that their productivity values can be compared among other physicians or in relation to their section average.

Lessons Learned

■ A prerequisite to beginning the design process is a thorough understanding of the business processes and available data sources.
■ Gap analysis is an important assessment exercise before the design process starts.
■ The design of a data model is an iterative process.
■ The key challenges during the data model design process are related to the availability of data, the cleansing of some existing data, and the

timing of the planned data updates. These key challenges need to be addressed and resolved, before the design process starts.

■ The data warehouse design should support scaling with additional software and hardware components, even if redundancy is not incorporated in the original implementation.

■ Generating some KPIs may require changes in the source systems to ensure that data are captured accurately. Because these changes may eventually require some change in the business process, business users must accept these changes before they are implemented.

Chapter 8

KPI Selection

Osama Alswailem

Contents

Key performance indicators, better known as KPIs, are core measures that decision makers use to gauge the performance of the healthcare enterprise in clinical, administrative, and financial areas. This chapter describes the process of KPI selection, from initial implementation through the operational phase of the data warehouse at King Faisal Specialist Hospital and Research Centre (KFSH&RC).

The life cycle of the KPIs starts with selection—including several phases of revision and approval—and continues through full implementation, successful utilization, and maintenance. KPI selection is crucial because it largely defines the potential success of the data warehouse project. Only with careful KPI selection can meaningful organizational performance monitoring and effective decision making be accomplished.

In fact, carefully selected and developed KPIs have helped KFSH&RC in not only performance improvement and decision making but also in accreditations such as JCIA, CAP, MAGNET, and HIMSS EMRAM.

Perspective

As quantitative metrics of performance, KPIs serve as a basis for objective, fact-based decisions and for measuring progress over time. As such, KPIs have been embraced by the key stakeholders and managers in our hospital as a means of driving performance improvement initiatives. We initially found the process of identifying KPIs painful, because it forced us to formulate a clear picture of our core processes that were largely ill-defined. We had to identify and compile objective data to formulate the indicators, which often meant instituting new measurement practices and even new data capturing mechanisms in the source systems. In the end, we realized that identifying and developing KPIs was primarily about addressing business issues and ways to monitor the performance of the organization and that technology was a necessary enabler.

We discovered that, in addition to a clear understanding of the clinical, administrative, and financial processes in our organization, formulating KPIs required us to have clear goals and performance requirements for each process. We had to identify quantitative and qualitative measures of process outcomes that could be compared with our goals and serve as the basis for adjusting processes and resources. A mnemonic that we found helpful in the KPI development process that summarizes these requirements is SMARTER: specific, measurable, achievable, realistic, timely, explainable, and relative.

Management Structure

As with most of major IT-supported initiatives, KPI development involved high-level executive sponsorship. Because of the need to involve stakeholders at multiple levels in our organization, management established a three-tiered structure during the time of project implementation.

The first tier, the Executive Committee, consisted of the executive management of the hospital. This committee, chaired by the chief executive officer (CEO), assumed the ultimate authority and responsibility for the project. The Executive Committee was charged with the review and approval of the system requirement specifications and project implementation plan, as well as providing management support. The Executive Committee was active in identifying high-level administrative KPIs, and quarterly meetings with the first tier were essential to keep up momentum.

The second tier in the management hierarchy, the Administrative Committee, consisted of key stakeholders at the department head level. This working committee, chaired by a physician with medical informatics training, played an active role in selecting, defining, and standardizing KPIs and related reports. In addition, the Administrative Committee established the priorities for deliverables, as well as ensured that these deliverables were consistent with hospital needs and conformed to policy, procedures, and processes.

The Administrative Committee was staffed with representatives from the office of the hospital's medical director, the major departments, the IT project manager, and the vendor's functional team leader. An external consultant experienced in selecting and defining KPIs in a large medical institution was also a member of the committee. The second tier was a bridge that connected the first and third tiers. Regular weekly meetings were instituted to monitor progress.

The third tier was composed of functional and technical team staff with informatics and application development experience. They were responsible for working directly with end users, often in tandem with a representative from the Administrative Committee, and reporting their progress to the entire Administrative Committee.

All three tiers were realigned to handle the post-implementation operational aspects of the data warehouse upon going live. The first two tiers were altered with minor modifications and the third tier was transformed completely. Changes to these structures are described in detail in Chapter 3, "Enterprise Environment," and in Chapter 10, "Post-implementation Organization Structure."

Working with End Users

The Administrative Committee assumed a major role in defining the KPI selection process. Initially, the committee was primarily involved in outreach, building awareness of the data warehouse project in the user community and the importance of end user involvement in selecting KPIs. As part of this effort, the committee formed a KPI subgroup that met with department heads to explain the concept of the data warehouse and its benefits. The committee also explored the goals, concerns, and expectations of the department heads. There were some cases where the departments had their own manual ways of gathering data or small programs that gave them the information they required. Educating the end users on the benefits of the data warehouse—in the early stages—was fundamental to reducing any resistance or reluctance.

Our aim was to create an open, collaborative environment where the KPI subgroup and department personnel could candidly discuss what processes to measure. We found it beneficial to use an outside consultant to help run the information-gathering sessions. An objective, apolitical perspective was especially useful in asking department heads for measures that would ultimately be used by hospital management to judge departmental performance.

The KPI subgroup faced two groups of department heads: those who clearly knew what processes and parameters they wanted to track and those who had difficulty translating their needs into indicators or informatics requirements. The second group required multiple sessions in which the KPI subgroup asked questions such as

- What are the problematic areas within your department that you would like to monitor?
- How do you currently measure and monitor the performance of your department with respect to international standards?
- How are information deficiencies and/or data gaps limiting the effectiveness of your department?
- Are there any new initiatives or performance improvement projects in place within your department that would benefit from assessment?
- Is your department seeking certification or accreditation? And if so, how is your department acquiring the data required by certification or accreditation groups?

To facilitate answers to these questions, the subgroup provided department heads with links to healthcare organizations (see Appendix I) and offered example KPIs as general guidelines. The subgroup was careful to introduce this information in a way that did not promote passive KPI selection.

Initial meetings were informative to both the KPI subgroup and the clinical and nonclinical department heads. The subgroup learned about the current state of departmental process management and the departments' use of information in decision making and was also in a position to assess the departments' facilities with computer tools and data-driven decision making—both useful in planning future department training for the data warehouse. Ensuring the free flow of information from department heads required the subgroup to reassure them about the confidentiality of their information and the value to the hospital in sharing information with management and other departments. It is worth noting that the departments that generated the data used in KPIs tended to choose familiar, existing metrics to track, although upper management and those in other departments preferred industry-standard KPI definitions.

Department heads were required to submit all the indicators needed for their departmental decision making. They were asked to provide a prioritized list for the indicators, beginning with the most important ones. In addition, they had to submit performance improvement initiatives with proper definitions, upper and lower bounds, and other parameters as defined by our standard KPI definition template (see Appendix I). The template contained 39 parameters, including definitions, calculations, and target populations, was developed by our functional consultant, and was approved by our Administrative Committee. If the department wanted more than 10 KPIs, they were required to submit a prioritized KPI wish list.

By the end of our exercise, 325 KPIs were identified by department heads and fully defined by our functional team (see Appendix VI). Although hospital management wanted to use as many KPIs as possible for the initial data warehouse implementation, our technical team and the vendor preferred a limited number of KPIs, with emphasis on building technical competency for future KPI development. After lengthy discussion, management decided to implement 45 KPIs. Preference was given to departments with high workloads, high risk, and/or significant process challenges. The 45 KPIs ultimately selected and approved by the Executive Committee for inclusion in the initial data warehouse implementation are listed in Table 8.1.

Upon completion of the project, KFSH&RC focused more on departmental outcomes than on KPIs based on user demands and interests, and produced hundreds of reports. Table 8.2 includes some of the important follow-on KPIs.

Since 2014, focus has been more on the development of KPIs and executive dashboards that are linked to the hospitals strategy. Table 8.3 provides examples of these strategic KPIs.

Table 8.4 shows the KPIs developed to evaluate physicians' productivity. Note that the indicators are a function of the physician's specialty.

Table 8.1   Initial KPI Implementation List

Emergency Room (ER)	Average waiting time
	Left without being seen rate
	Revisits to ER within 72 hours
	ER admissions
	ER discharges
	ER mortality
Oncology	Physician load
	Total number of discharges
	Breast cancer survival rate
Nursing	Turnover distribution
Radiology	Report turnaround
Pharmacy	Days in inventory
	Out-of-stock rate
Pathology	Pathology lab results turnaround time
	Blood product wastage rate
	Blood product transfusion rate
Eligibility	Turnaround time for accepting new patients
Appointments	Patient clinic visit waiting time
	Patient waiting time
	Outpatient confirmed appointment cancellation rate
Human Resources	Employee cost
	Staff stability rate
	Sick leave cost rate
Payroll	Paid leave to regular time
	Saudization (staffed by Saudi citizens)
Finance	Asset turnover
	Accounts receivable rate
	Patient accounts receivable turnover
	Quick ratio

(Continued)

Table 8.1 (Continued)   Initial KPI Implementation List

Logistics	Total number of zero-stock days
	Inventory turnover rate
Global	Average length of stay
	Length of stay
	Average daily census
	Beds
	Admissions
	Discharges
	Bed turnover rate
	Patient days
	Occupancy rate
	Hospital mortality rate
	Readmission to Critical Care Unit
	Overtime rate
	Staff turnover rate
	Sick time rate

Table 8.5 lists executive dashboard indicators that have been developed for the CEO and the chief operating officers (COOs) of KFSH&RC's main hospital and Jeddah branch.

Challenges

Developing relevant, feasible, and reliable KPIs required our staff to overcome several conceptual, functional, and technical challenges. We had to educate the department heads about the difference between abstract metrics and complex, multifaceted KPIs. Metrics, such as length of stay, exist independently of the manner in which they are collected and used. A KPI based on length of stay, in contrast, is precisely defined, associated with an action plan, and assigned an owner. The owner is responsible for monitoring the KPI in terms of performance and utility and must suggest modifications in the calculation or composition of the KPI as detailed in the action

Table 8.2   Follow-On KPI Implementation List

ER	Daily encounter
	Overtime rate
	Physician load
Nursing	Falls prevalence
	CE (continuing education) units
	Pressure ulcer prevalence
	Variance NHPPD (nursing hours per patient day)
Radiology	Radiologist availability index
	Dictation turnaround time
	Equipment utilization rate
	Overtime rate
	Radiologist productivity index
	Total available staff hours
	Outpatient wait time for routine appointment
	Inpatient wait time for procedure—Radiology
	Verification turnaround around time—Radiology
Pharmacy	Medication disposal rate
	Average wait times
	YTD (year to date) cost
	Average number of pharmaceuticals unavailable per day
Pathology	Outpatient waiting time—Phlebotomy
	Number of blood products transfused
	Total number of blood products modified
	Total blood products available in the blood bank
	Specimen delivery time
	Modified blood product rate

(Continued)

Table 8.2 (Continued)   Follow-On KPI Implementation List

Cardiology	Admissions
	Procedures in unit—CICU (Cardiac Intensive Care Unit)
	Unplanned return rate to OR
	Mortality rate
	Readmission rate
MSICU (Medical/ Surgical Intensive Care Unit)	Mortality rate
	Readmission rate
PICU (Pediatric Intensive Care Unit)	Mortality rate
	Readmission rate
NICU (Neonatal Intensive Care Unit)	Mortality rate
	Readmission rate
OR	OR procedure performance rate
	OR cancellation rate
	Average OR turnaround time
	Scheduled OR utilization rate
	Total number of anesthesia hours per anesthesiologist
	OR utilization—after scheduled hours
Quality of care	Total number of harm events
Medical records	Total number of delinquent medical records
Eligibility	Accepted new patient rate
Human resources	Head count
	Employee distribution status
	Number of terminated employees
	Gender distribution
	International hire distribution
	Staff turnover rate
	Full-time equivalent (FTE)
	Primary workforce

(*Continued*)

Table 8.2 (Continued)   Follow-On KPI Implementation List

Payroll	Overtime rate
	Overtime to paid leave rate
	Sick leave to overtime rate
	Sick time rate
	Staff turnover rate
	Unpaid leave to regular time
Finance	Budget variance rate
	Revenue generation
	Payroll expense by department
	Rate of return on assets
Supply chain	Time taken for requisitions to reach to procurement department
	Time taken for approved purchase order items delivered by the vendor
	End user request turnaround time
	Purchase order processing rate
Global	Outpatient wait time for routine appointment
	Inpatient wait time for procedure
	Number of patients with length of stay greater or less than 30 and 60 days, respectively

plan. Furthermore, the action plan is formulated when the KPI is defined, in advance of when it is actually needed.

Conceptual Challenges

It was difficult to determine the KPIs' priority in the implementation queue, ownership, and threshold values that would require action. Although we knew that the development of KPIs should be tied to organizational or specific departmental strategies, we discovered a lack of transparency in strategies because of organizational politics. For example, a source of numerous conflicts was the desire of department heads and staff to dismiss KPIs that might indicate their department was underperforming. Instead, they favored

Table 8.3   Strategic KPIs

Access to care	Accepted cases
	Total cases referred
	New patient (NP) first encounter <2 weeks
	ER waiting time to be seen
	ER admission waiting time
	Transfers out of hospital
Productivity	Outpatient Department clinic visits
	Oncology treatment area visits
	DEM (Department of Emergency Medicine) visits
	OR cases (hours)
	Number of transplants
	Cardiac surgeries
	Day medical visits
	Day surgeries
Patient experience	Responsiveness of hospital staff
	Pain management
	Discharge information
	Clinic waiting time satisfaction
Quality of care	Sentinel events
	Percentage of near-miss events
	Pressure ulcers
	Falls with injury
	Number of safety reports
Hospital-acquired infections	Hand hygiene
	Central line (CLABSI – Central Line Associated Bloodstream Infections)
	Urinary catheters (CAUTI – Catheter Associated Urinary Tract Infection)
	Surgical site infection (SSI)

(Continued)

Table 8.3 (Continued)   Strategic KPIs

Education and training	CME hours provided
	Number of participants in online courses
	Life support–certified participants
	Medical trainees
Research	Publications
	Approved research proposals
	Cites per paper
	Number of patent applications
Human Resources	Number of employees
	Voluntary attrition rate
Finance	Generated revenue (millions) (USD)
	Manpower cost (millions) (USD)
	Average cost per adjusted patient day
	Gross margin (%)

nonstrategic KPIs that reflected high performance. We found a diverse KPI selection team composed of clinical, medical, finance, logistic, research, and IT specialists helpful in this regard. We also relied on a senior hospital administrator to drive the initiative, cast tie-breaking votes, and set the cultural tone.

Functional Challenges

A key role of the Administrative Committee was to establish a clear and agreed-upon KPI identification and selection process to balance the interests of our healthcare enterprise with those of individual department heads. There were many instances where the needs of the organization were at odds with those of one or more departments. KPIs with an organizational focus incorporated departmental indicators, thus making the KPI also useful at the department level. Otherwise, this could have had a major impact on the actual utilization of the KPIs among the different parties.

Another functional challenge was whether to adhere to KPI standards and, if so, which standards to use. Established, international standards for names, definitions, formulas, filters, and exclusion and inclusion criteria for

Table 8.4 Physician Productivity KPIs

Domain	Category	Sub-Category	Indicator Name
Clinical	Administrative		Committee chairman
			Committee member
	Operational		Discharge from clinic
			Outreach patients seen
			Same day OR (inpatient)
			Same day OR (outpatient)
			Discharges
			Uniquely attended patients
			First available new follow-up (NF)
			First available new patient (NP)
			DMU and DPU visits
	Productivity	Inpatient	Inpatient consultations
			Patient days
			Discharges
			Admissions
		Others	Closed sessions
			Overtime hours

(Continued)

Table 8.4 (Continued)   Physician Productivity KPIs

Domain	Category	Sub-Category	Indicator Name
			On call sessions weekends
			Open sessions
			On call sessions weekdays
			DEM visits
			Home health care visits
			FU seen
			Outpatient consultations
			NF seen
			NP seen
			Emergency consultations
			DEM physician note
		Procedures	Pain procedures
			Completed OR
			OR hours
			Dialysis procedures
			Ortho procedures
			ANS completed in OR

(Continued)

Table 8.4 (Continued) Physician Productivity KPIs

Domain	Category	Sub-Category	Indicator Name
			ANS (Anesthesias) completed in OR hours
			Ophthalmology procedures
			Radiology verified reports
			Chemo therapy unique patients
			Endoscopy procedures
			IVF (In Vitro Fertilization) procedures
			ORL (Oral) procedures
			Vag deliveries
			HeartNet finalized reports
			Radiation therapy unique patients
			BMT (Bone Marrow Transplant) unique patients
			Dental procedures
			Derma procedures
			Lab verified orders
			Neurophysiology reports
			Carestream R4 dental procedures
			CATH (Catheterization) procedures

(Continued)

Table 8.4 (Continued) Physician Productivity KPIs

Domain	Category	Sub-Category	Indicator Name
			EP procedures
			Echo procedures
			BMT transfusions
			Radiation therapy sessions
			Chemotherapy sessions
	Research		Research proposals as co-investigator
			Publications as first author
			Research proposals as principal investigator
			Publications as co author
Financial			Total physician RVUs
Quality			Inpatient Peds satisfaction
			Average delinquent records
			Re-admissions same service within 30 days thru EMS
			OR estimated blood loss
			Re-admissions same service within 3 days
			Return to OR within 30 days
			HCAHPS physician positive answers

(Continued)

Table 8.4 (Continued)   Physician Productivity KPIs

Domain	Category	Sub-Category	Indicator Name
			HCAHPS physician answers
			Outpatient satisfaction SMS (Short Messaging Service) positive answers
			Outpatient satisfaction SMS all answers
			Inpatient Peds satisfaction positive answers
			Inpatient Peds satisfaction all answers
			Eligibility referred cases
			Eligibility referred cases (unique)
			Eligibility referrals response average min
			Eligibility referrals response total min
			Average OR estimated blood loss
			HCAHP satisfaction
			Average length of stay based on discharge days
			Re-admissions within 3 days
			Re-admissions within 30 days thru EMS
			Patients died within 15 days of surgery
			OR delayed reason = surgeon delay
			Deaths
			Patients died after 15 days of surgery

Table 8.5   Executive Dashboard KPIs

Domain	Indicator
Emergency	Patients waiting to be seen by doctor
	Patients flagged for admissions
	Patients flagged for admissions with assigned bed
	Last 24 hour emergency visits by acuity level
	Last 10 hour emergency visits
Inpatient	Actual occupancy
	Last 3 days mortality
	Admission vs. discharge PM and AM
	Patients length of stay
OR	Surgeries scheduled today
	Surgeries beyond their scheduled time or started late
	Canceled surgeries that were scheduled today
	Completed surgeries today so far
	Last 7 days surgery
	Last 7 days cases of inpatient admitted for surgery
Waiting time	Pharmacy tickets by hour
	Pharmacy average waiting time last 3 hours
	Laboratory tickets by hour
	Laboratory average waiting time last 3 hours
Outpatient	Scheduled appointments today
	Appointments by slot type
	Physicians open and closed sessions
	Top canceled by specialty
	Top no show by specialty
	Standard slots scheduled vs. checked

(Continued)

Table 8.5 (Continued) Executive Dashboard KPIs

Domain	*Indicator*
Human Resources	Active primary employees
	Primary employee MTD (month-to-date) terminations
	Primary employee MTD hires
	Primary positions
	Top job titles with percentage of vacancies out of FTEs is ≥ 15%
	Percentage of vacancies for nursing job category
	Percentage of vacancies for technical health allied job category
	Percentage of vacancies for physicians job category
	Number of active primary staff on leave today
	On duty vs. on leave
Supply chain	YTD requisitions approved by users' departments
	YTD approved POs (Purchase Orders)
	YTD received shipments
	Out-of-stock pharmaceuticals
	Supplies budget vs. YTD received
Finance	Invoices consuming current year budget
	All paid invoices
	All outstanding invoices
	Employees not receiving their salary of month on time
	YTD collected cash
	Annual allocated budget
	YTD posted charges
	Manpower YTD expenses

KPIs seemed intuitively obvious to use, but many of our hospital departments were using nonstandard measures of performance. There were sometimes multiple formulas used to calculate the same measures within the hospital. Simply dropping these local standards in deference to international standards would have made it difficult for department heads and hospital management to compare changes in performance.

Our greatest concern was with our Medical Record Department, the keeper of hospital statistics and report generator. When we began our data warehouse initiative, the Medical Records Department was using an outdated version of the American Health Information Management Association (AHIMA) standards. In the end, we were successful in compiling a list of KPI reference sources, based on recommendations from them, our data warehouse consultant, and a compilation of international benchmark standards used by hospitals in North America and Europe.

Instead of having one reference definition source for all KPIs, the Administrative Committee chose to have a number of references ranked from the most to the least preferred (Table 8.6). Departments were allowed to use the KPI definitions that best suited their ongoing operations. In contrast, we selected reference definitions for global KPIs that reflected the needs of the organization, including our desire to benchmark our performance with that of similar hospitals in North America and Europe.

Table 8.6 Ranked KPI Reference Sources

Rank	Source
1	American Health Information Management Association (AHIMA)
2	American Hospital Association (AHA)
3	Centers for Medicare and Medicaid Services (CMS)/The Joint Commission
4	Agency for Healthcare Research and Quality (AHRQ)
5	National Health Service (NHS)
6	Specialty-specific sources (United States) a) American Colleges and Boards—e.g., College of American Pathologists (CAP) b) Professional Societies—e.g., Radiology Business Management Association (RBMA)
7	Quality organizations (see Appendix VI)
	Charting (dashboard) standard: *Tools for Performance Measurement in Health Care: A Quick Reference Guide*, Oakbrook Terrace, IL: Joint Commission Resources, 2002.
	Financial definition source: Zelman, W., et al., *Financial Management of Health Care Organizations: An Introduction to Fundamental Tools, Concepts, and Applications*, 2nd ed., Cornwall, U.K.: Blackwell, 2003.

The Administrative Committee assigned a focus subgroup to facilitate standardization, whether through the identification of reference sources or to freeze legacy definitions. In cases where legacy definitions differed from newly adopted KPI definitions, a provision or adjustment was made such that the original definition was incorporated into the new definition. The new KPI definition contained both new and legacy versions and produced two values: one for comparison with historic data and one for benchmarking with other hospitals and standards organizations.

Technical Challenges

To facilitate knowledge transfer, most of the initial KPIs were developed by our technical staff working closely with the vendor. In order for our technical staff to gain experience working with the range of source systems in our enterprise, KPIs were identified that required data access from a particular source application, as opposed to fulfilling a functional need. In retrospect, this diversion from the SMARTER approach to identifying and developing was detrimental to our data warehouse implementation.

Our original vision was for the functional team to specify KPIs based on the needs of the organization and the department heads, with the underlying, difficult assumption that data in the various applications were both available and accessible. In reality, these assumptions were often invalid. The functional team invested time and resources identifying KPIs the technical team could not deliver, either because data were not available or there was no process in place to capture the needed data in the source applications.

For example, the majority of initial KPIs required data from our Cerner Integrated Clinical Information System (ICIS), the pillar application at our institution. This presented an enormous technical challenge to our technical team because the vendor lacked expertise with ICIS; the nearly 4,000 tables had to be manually searched for relevant data supportive of the selected KPIs. The technical groups determined that although there were placeholders in ICIS for much of the required data, there was no process in place to actually acquire some of the data necessary to construct several KPIs.

Fortunately, data in the ICIS system were accessible by the technical team, but toward the end of implementation, we discovered issues with the accuracy of data. We attribute these errors to our lack of knowledge of the ICIS system and, by extension, our failure to insist that the vendor provide an expert technical resource for the ICIS work. We could not reach an agreement with Cerner for help in understanding the underlying data model.

Many of the KPIs related to finance and supply chain management required data from our Oracle enterprise resource planning (ERP) application. This application, used by administration, financial affairs, and logistics, incorporates about 3,000 tables. Unlike the case with ICIS, the vendor proved knowledgeable about the inner workings of the ERP application, even though our ERP installation was heavily customized to mirror our internal processes, as opposed to industry best practices. As a result, the vendor was tasked with understanding the undocumented modifications to the ERP application and creating custom methods of extracting data as part of the KPI development process. Many of the modifications are now documented as a result of this effort.

The third category of applications that provided source data for KPIs, the proprietary systems, also presented challenges to our technical group. For example, our Operating Room scheduling and utilization management applications held key data required for KPIs. We lacked connectivity with and accessibility to the underlying databases, so data extraction was not possible and we were forced to temporarily drop several of our most important KPIs.

Because of the importance of KPIs such as Operating Room (OR) procedure performance rate, OR cancellation rate, average OR turnaround time, and total number of anesthesia hours per anesthesiologist, we moved to upgrade the systems to open databases. Our OR scheduling and utilization management application was replaced by a Cerner SurgiNet component as part of the ICIS phase 2 implementation in early 2010. KPIs that were dropped earlier were readdressed, and many were subsequently implemented in our data warehouse.

Over the years since the initial implementation of our data warehouse, what we have found is that a bottom-up approach is more effective, where department leaders—as opposed to department heads—play a major role in the identification and selection of KPIs. This approach not only encourages ownership but also promotes the utilization of KPIs. A successful KPI selection process satisfies the needs of both department leaders and department heads and results in better long-term KPI utilization.

Lessons Learned

■ The KPI selection process should include clear action plans set by the requesters to effectively utilize the KPI.

■ The action plan should address the justification for KPI implementation, the validating authority, the audiences for the KPI, the life span of the KPI, and a periodic review of the effectiveness and utilization of the KPI.

■ The organization should have a strong data-driven performance improvement culture.

■ It is imperative to quickly build trust in the data warehouse system among the user community and hospital executives.

■ Invest more energy in acquiring technical knowledge than in functional detailed analysis.

■ Secure a vendor with technical knowledge of the source systems before beginning work.

■ A bottom-up approach is effective in the KPI identification and selection process.

■ User requests for KPI development should include action and utilization plans.

■ An agreed-upon reference for KPI standards is important for user acceptance and buy-in.

Chapter 9

Implementation

Enam UL Hoque

Contents

Final implementation of any IT project is a misnomer. In reality, it marks the beginning of maintenance, active user support, and a variety of activities that drive and encourage the users to buy in. This chapter describes the highlights of the implementation process.

Scope

The major activities performed during the implementation phase of our data warehouse were the ETL build, the end user application (e.g., OLAP) build, user acceptance testing (UAT), and sign-off. To better manage the project and deliverables, we limited the initial build to include only 45 KPIs. The remaining 146 KPIs were to be built upon the successful rollout of the initial 45 KPIs.

ETL Build

The main task for the ETL build was to develop and execute ETL Scripts for the extracting, cleansing, transforming, and loading of data into the data warehouse. Script development was based on the physical data model and ETL design document, with additional ETL build scripts for standard data quality checking during the transformation and data-cleansing process. The initial ETL build processes also encompassed the following activities:

■ Connections were made to 11 source systems, including our mainframe and systems running UNIX, Linux, and Windows.
■ Staging operational data store (ODS) and warehouse database schemas were built.
■ 185 staging tables were created.
■ 16 ODS fact tables were created.
■ 45 dimension tables were created in the production data warehouse.
■ 98 fact tables were created in the production data warehouse.
■ 233 Informatica mappings were scripted.
■ 36 Informatica sessions were run daily to extract data from source systems to the staging area.
■ 14 Informatica sessions were run to extract, transform, and load data from source system to tables in the ODS schema.
■ 79 Informatica sessions were used for transforming and loading data from the staging area to the production data warehouse.
■ 798 unit/integration test cases were built and executed.

As part of the extraction, transformation, and loading (ETL) build process, data transformations were individually tested. Errors were logged during the ETL build process using Informatica mappings in the Informatica server and session error log files. Scripts written as part of the ETL build electronically distributed the log files to support personnel for review and resolution.

Online Analytical Processing (OLAP) Build

Our primary OLAP development activities evolved around transforming the OLAP design into cubes, reports, scorecards, and dashboards using Cognos Business Intelligence tools: ReportNet for dynamic reports, Cubes for analytical reports, Metrics Manager for scorecards, and Visualizer for dashboards.

The highlights of the OLAP build process for the initial 45 KPIs included the development of

- 21 cubes based on subject areas
- 16 framework models
- 19 packages
- 23 scorecards
- 7 dashboards
- 77 reports
- 2,000 unit/integration test cases

The typical OLAP build addresses different user needs and perspectives. Power users may want to drill down to the atomic level. Middle managers may prefer the summarized and aggregated data. Executives may place more value on the bird's eye view of data through scorecards and customizable dashboards. Unfortunately, we missed the opportunity to address the myriad needs and perspectives of our clinicians, administrators, and researchers. We attribute the lack of user satisfaction and level of use of the initial 45 KPIs to this oversight. Our users were not ready for sophisticated analytics in cubes with drill-up/-down/-across and multidimensional analysis. They were only ready for a simple one-dimensional operational report. With vigorous training, our executive-level users still prefer one-dimensional operational reports. So, we further developed power users in key areas to consume sophisticated analytics and help our executives with their reporting needs through the advanced features of analytical cubes.

User Acceptance Testing

UAT and end-user training are customarily performed prior to deployment and sign-off. UAT touches the results of every data warehouse process, from loading data through ETL to accessing data through OLAP deliverables. Testing was complicated because much of the data from the source system was not loaded into the warehouse and the data that were loaded were often transformed through ETL. As a result, direct comparisons between data in the source systems and those in the data warehouse were difficult.

We formed a joint team with representatives from the vendor to perform UAT exercises. A total of 624 UAT cases were developed and executed by the team. Many technical defects were raised and resolved in a structured and iterative process. However, as noted previously, testing revealed short-comings in the requirement definitions. This was reflected in low end-user confidence and buy-in of the data warehouse during the initial stage of the implementation. The shortcomings in the requirement definitions required revisiting the initial design, which delayed the deployment of OLAP deliverables.

User acceptance was also negatively impacted by the lack of user training. Business intelligence tools bring a new analytical dimension to reports that require structured and extensive end-user training. End-user training is usually planned in parallel with the UAT exercise and conducted upon completion of UAT. However, due to the shortcomings uncovered by the UAT exercise, training activities were cancelled.

To enhance end user acceptance of the data warehouse deliverables, we formed an Administrative Committee with the directive of executive management. The mandate of this committee was to address and resolve all shortcomings in the data warehouse.

Lessons Learned

- The success of the implementation phase depends on the soundness of the planning and design phase. Implementation is straightforward if planning and design conclude successfully with technical and application architecture well in place.
- Failure to address the different needs and perspectives of the user community in the OLAP build will result in poor user acceptance.
- End-user training is crucial for acceptance and buy-in to use the analytics and reports produced out of the data warehouse.

Chapter 10

Post-implementation Organizational Structure

Enam UL Hoque and Hamad Al-Daig

Contents

Upon successful implementation of our data warehouse project, the issue of management structure for ongoing operation of the data warehouse was raised several times by various bodies within King Faisal Specialist Hospital and Research Centre (KFSH&RC). To address the overall management issue as it relates to the operational aspects of the data warehouse, executive management established three distinct structures with clearly defined charges. This chapter describes those organizational structures as well as the charges, roles, and responsibilities of those associated with the operation of the data warehouse.

    The organizational structure for any major undertaking within an organization is an evolving process. As such, KFSH&RC's structure is evolving as we continue operationalizing our data warehouse deliverables.

    Evolving from project to operation mode for data warehouse development required proper planning in terms of organizational structure, the deployment of manpower with the right skill sets, and defining the roles and responsibilities of all involved parties. During the operational phase of the implemented data warehouse, KFSH&RC faced some challenges in the following areas:

- Participation of key decision makers
- Commitment to dedicate adequate resources
- Functional expertise to define requirements
- Standards to follow for the definition of key performance indicators (KPIs)

The participation of key decision makers is paramount in the development of a data warehouse. The ground reality is that most decision makers are busy with their day-to-day work. Allocating the proper time to do justice to data warehouse development was putting extra pressure on many decision makers during the project implementation. So, the executive management had to balance the involvement and participation of decision makers. Revamping of the organizational structures and players within those structures is one of the steps taken by upper management to address this issue.

Dedicating adequate in-house resources to take over from the vendor upon completion of the project was an issue raised to executive management to take appropriate action. In the technical area, management supported the creation of two operational organizational structures within HITA, which will be discussed in more detail later in this chapter.

The functional expertise to define requirements is an important factor for data warehouse development. Since the completion of this project, KFSH&RC has struggled to build an ideal structure with functional expertise due to several reasons. The main reason is that it is extremely difficult to find in-house functional experts with wide hospital background and experience. Secondly, it takes time to develop said personnel into functional experts. KFSH&RC tried but the hospital had faced a retention problem with resignations and transfers within the organization. Despite these challenges, we are continuing our data warehouse development activities, adding new analytics, scorecards, dashboards, and reports.

Some of the challenges around "Standards to follow for definitions of KPI" had been alleviated through our alliance with Premier, Inc. The partnership was to facilitate internal productivity analysis and benchmark our hospital with those in the United States. As Premier, Inc. has many industry-standard definitions, KFSH&RC's management decided to adopt all applicable definitions into our data warehouse deliverables.

Management Structures

The executive management of KFSH&RC realigned the Data Warehouse Executive Committee to include membership as in Table 10.1.

The charges of the Data Warehouse Executive Committee are as follows:

- Oversee and monitor the scope of the data warehouse system at KFSH&RC (General Organization).
- Standardize definitions and formulae for any future deliverables (KPIs and reports) of the data warehouse.

Table 10.1   Data Warehouse Executive Committee Membership

Chief executive officer	Chairman
Chief information officer	Coordinator
Chief operating officer, Riyadh	Member
Chief operating officer, Jeddah branch	Member
Chief administrative officer	Member
Chief financial officer	Member
Chief clinical auditor	Member
Executive director, Medical and Clinical Affairs	Member
Executive director, Administrative Services	Member
Executive director, Research Centre	Member
Executive director, Supply Chain Management	Member
Deputy executive director, Medical and Clinical Affairs	Member
Director, Organization and Management	Member
Director, Quality Management	Member
Director, Medical and Clinical Informatics	Member
Chairman, Biostatistics, Epidemiology, and Scientific Computing	Member
Director, Information Technology Services, Jeddah branch	Member

■ Approve the evaluation criteria for the data warehouse system and standardize definition criteria for deliverables.
■ Approve multidepartmental global reports.
■ Provide support and guidance to any working group(s) and/or any other subcommittee(s) formed in due course.
■ Resolve any other related issues/concerns related to the data warehouse system.

The Data Warehouse Executive Committee is to meet quarterly to provide overall guidance and address issues and concerns on an ad hoc basis.

The executive management of KFSH&RC had also established the Enterprise Reports Committee (ERC) as an oversight body to handle new development as well as to handle the post-implementation operational aspects of the data warehouse.

Enterprise Reports Committee

Since the establishment of the ERC, it has been chaired by an executive with wide hospital management experience within KFSH&RC. The charges of this group mandated by executive management includes the following:

■ Standardize the definitions and formulae for future data warehouse deliverables.
■ Assure that these deliverables are consistent with hospital needs and conform to policies, procedures, and processes.
■ Set priorities for future deliverables.
■ Address and help resolve data and process gap issues related to source systems.
■ Promote and market the deliverables of the data warehouse.
■ Develop policies regarding access management and all other related matters.

The ERC includes representatives from every key area of the hospital. Weekly meetings are held by the ERC to carry out its charges. In addition, it invites other representatives of hospital operations, on an ad hoc basis, to the committee's weekly meetings.

Members of the ERC include those listed in Table 10.2.

Executive management also approved the creation of two new permanent organizational units within Information Technology Affairs (ITA): Enterprise

Table 10.2 Enterprise Reports Committee Membership

Chief clinical auditor	Chairman
Manager, Enterprise Reporting Services	Coordinator
Deputy chief information officer	Member
Director, Medical and Clinical Informatics	Member
Director, Patient Affairs	Member
Representative, Financial Affairs	Member
Representative, Medical and Clinical Affairs	Member
Representative, Administrative Affairs	Member
Representative, Supply Chain Management	Member
Representative, Nursing Affairs	Member
Representative, Quality Resource Management	Member
Representatives, Healthcare Information Technology Affairs	Member

Reporting Services (ERS) and Enterprise Data Architecture (EDA), under the IT infrastructure division.

The ERS structure addresses the maintenance of existing data warehouse deliverables and develops and deploys additional analytics, dashboards, scorecards, and reports needed by user departments.

Enterprise Reporting Services

While the overarching goal of ERS is to maintain and retain the skill sets and experience gained, the primary mandate of ERS is to provide a "single source of truth" through data warehouse deliverables in a timely manner. In practice, this translates to the development of deliverables comprised of simple-to-complex analytics, reports, dashboards, and scorecards. In the process of creating ERS, HITA clearly defined the stakeholders of the services and their roles, as well as processes to support efficient hospital-wide reporting.

ERS is the delivery and execution body that maintains the existing deliverables of the data warehouse, as well as develops and deploys new deliverables needed by the hospital. The primary role of the ERS team is to streamline the entire process of report generation, bridging with the user community to ensure a smooth transition from requirement gathering, designing, and report development to the user acceptance of reports.

Detailed roles and responsibilities of the ERS include

- Assisting hospital departments in defining operational and/or analytical reports
- Defining confidentiality and security needs in coordination with related stakeholders and the technical team
- Identifying process, system, or data gaps and formulating strategies to overcome these gaps
- Executing technical design and development tasks
- Helping stakeholders with data validation
- Facilitating user acceptance in coordination with related stakeholders
- Creating and applying security structures in production
- Marketing the deliverables of the data warehouse
- Providing technical support

To carry out the roles and responsibilities highlighted above, ERS was structured as shown in Figure 10.1 under the direct supervision of HITA management.

Enterprise Data Architecture

EDA's structure was created to address data modeling, ETL, and metadata creation in support of enterprise-wide data integration as well as data warehouse deliverables.

Executive management supported the creation of the EDA unit to take responsibility for the overall design, organization, and assessment of enterprise data structures. This unit is expected to implement and improve the current data management strategy and enterprise data architecture by applying a combination of industry best practices and

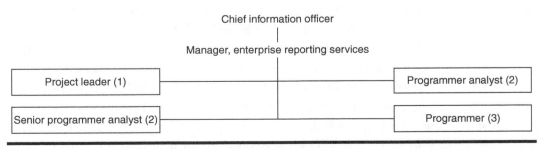

Figure 10.1 Enterprise reporting services structure.

innovation, and learned solutions through the implementation of our data warehouse. The enterprise data architecture is in the process-building stage at KFSH&RC.

Detailed roles and responsibilities of the EDA include

- Ensuring that all enterprise database applications fit into an enterprise data model that minimizes the duplication of data
- Ensuring logical data access
- Providing accurate and consistent synchronized information across all data environments
- Directing the design, development, review, documentation, and implementation of data models
- Creating metadata structures for enterprise-wide relational database applications
- Leading the data integration architecture
- Supporting OLAP, OLTP, and other data warehouse applications through ETL operation
- Developing and maintaining an enterprise data architecture roadmap based on business requirements

To carry out the roles and responsibilities highlighted above, the EDA unit was structured as shown in Figure 10.2 under the head of IT Infrastructure division of HITA.

Hospital Departments: Roles and Responsibilities for the Data Warehouse

Hospital departments, the main consumer of data warehouse deliverables, have major roles to play in cooperation with the ERC and ERS.

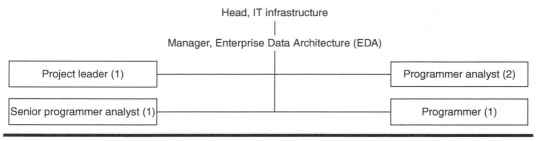

Figure 10.2   Enterprise data architecture unit structure.

These roles and responsibilities include

- Requesting and owning data warehouse deliverables
- Providing definitions of KPIs and measures
- Preparing functional documents in coordination with ERS
- Validating data warehouse deliverables in coordination with ERS
- Providing formal acceptance for data warehouse deliverables
- Conducting periodical reviews for usability and accuracy in coordination with ERS

Major areas of our hospital such as Medical and Clinical Affairs, Laboratory, Pharmacy, Radiology, Financial Services, and Supply Chain Management have dedicated resources as data coordinator(s), and those resources were encouraged to take on the roles and responsibilities stated previously. For smaller departments, not having any dedicated data coordinator, members within the department were oriented to carry out these roles and responsibilities.

Lesson Learned

- The organizational structure of the data warehouse should be reflective of the institution's own corporate culture and functions.
- The participation of key stakeholders is of paramount importance.
- The involvement of user departments for data validation is extremely crucial.
- The roles and responsibilities should be clearly defined for each functioning body so they may carry out the operational aspects of the data warehouse.
- Definitions must be standardized with international reference source(s).
- Dedicating adequate resources is extremely important to the success of data warehouse development.

Chapter 11

Data Warehouse Report Life Cycle

Enam UL Hoque

Contents

Upon completion of the initial phase of the data warehouse project, Enterprise Reporting Services (ERS) felt the need to define the data warehouse report life cycle, from report generation to report retirement. This chapter outlines the data warehouse report life cycle defined by ERS.

Requesting New Reports

Requests for new reports are submitted to ERS. All requests are approved at the chairman/department head level and prioritized if there are multiple new report requests pending for the same department. Upon receipt of a request, ERS does the following:

1. Performs an initial feasibility assessment, working with the requesting department and related functional areas. Notifies requesting department of the report feasibility.
2. Confirms the definition, criterion, and functional analysis with requesting department and related functional areas.
3. Designs and develops reports.
4. Facilitates the validation of reports by the requesting department in coordination with functional analysts.
5. Obtains formal acceptance from the requesting department. Accepted reports are moved to the production environment.
6. Provides authorized users access to reports.
7. Provides the necessary training to authorized users.
8. Adds the report to the report catalog and announces its availability to authorized users.

For multidepartmental and global report requests, steps 1 and 2 are completed and the results are forwarded to the Enterprise Reports Committee (ERC) for prioritization and approval. The process flow of new report generation is shown in Figure 11.1.

Requesting Changes to Existing Reports

Change requests to existing reports are prioritized and submitted to the chairman/department head for approval. Upon approval and receipt of the written request, ERS does the following:

1. Performs a feasibility assessment of the requested change in coordination with the related functional areas. The requestor is notified if the change is not feasible.
2. Makes the requested change.
3. Facilitates the validation of reports by user departments in coordination with functional analysts.
4. Obtains formal acceptance of changes to move reports into the production environment.
5. Retrains authorized users, if necessary.
6. Updates the report catalog and announces the availability of the new report to authorized users.

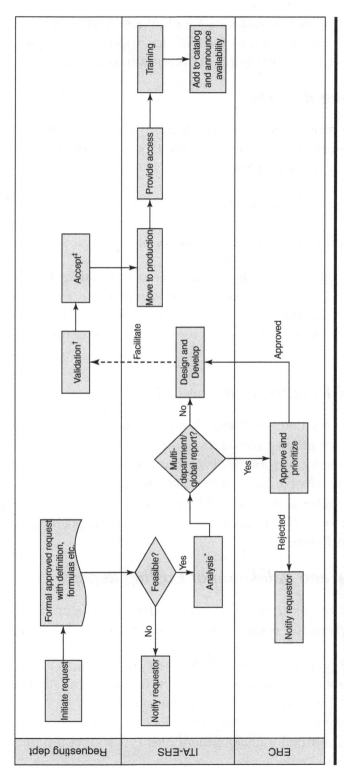

Figure 11.1 New report generation process.

* Analysis may require the involvement of all related stakeholders.

† Validation may require the involvement of key department(s) and the ERC, particularly for multidepartmental/global reports.

‡ Acceptance is to be given at the executive director level of the relevant department.

Upon completion of step 1, requests for changes of multidepartmental and global reports are forwarded to the ERC for approval. The process flow of handling changes to an existing report is shown in Figure 11.2.

Removal of Existing Reports

Removal of existing reports must be approved by the chairman/department head through written communication to ERS. Upon receipt of written communication, ERS does the following:

1. Removes the report from the production environment.
2. Removes user access.
3. Updates the catalog and announces the removal.

Requests for the removal of existing multidepartmental and global reports are forwarded to the ERC for approval. If the removal request is rejected by the ERC, the requestor is notified; otherwise, ERS performs the three steps defined above. The process flow for the removal of an existing report is shown in Figure 11.3.

Escalation of Problems/Issues to the ERC

Any stakeholder can escalate problems/issues to the ERC by addressing the committee coordinator at least two days prior to a scheduled committee meeting. The resolution of problems/issues at the level of working bodies, however, without the involvement of the ERC, is encouraged. Decisions of the ERC are communicated to stakeholders, who are charged with implementing those decisions. The process flow of escalating problems/issues to the ERC is shown in Figure 11.4.

Periodical Review and Validation of Existing Reports

Reports are periodically reviewed and validated to reflect current hospital operations. The steps of the review and validation process are as follows:

1. For operational reports, the owner department conducts a review of relevance and usability. Data validation is performed annually or as often as specified by the functional documentation.
2. For analytical reports, the owner of the KPI is required to conduct a review as per the functional document and to conduct an annual data validation.

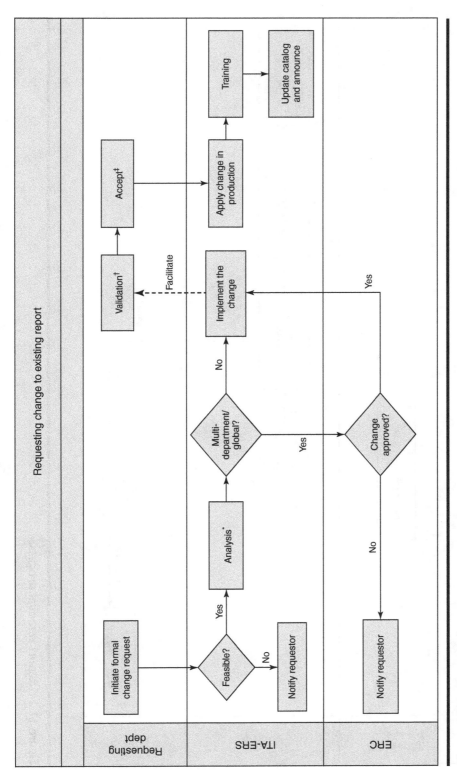

Figure 11.2 Report change process.

* Analysis may require the involvement of all related stakeholders.

† Validation may require the involvement of key department(s) and ERS, particularly for multidepartmental/global reports.

‡ Acceptance is given at the executive director level of the relevant department.

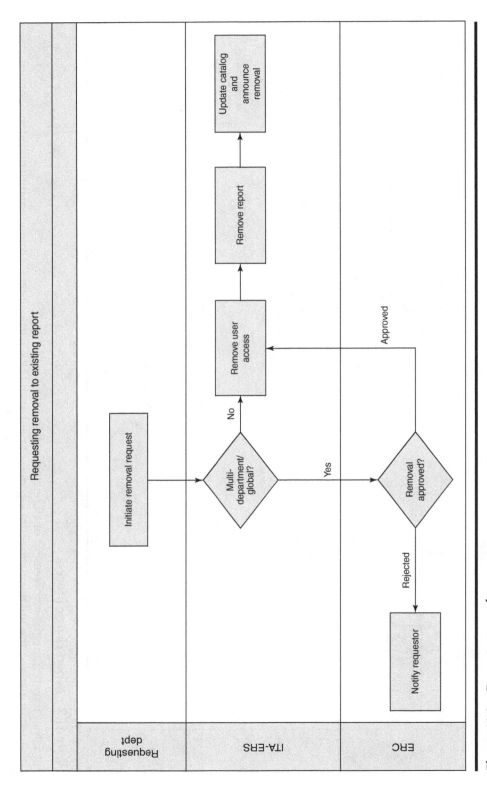

Figure 11.3 Report removal process.

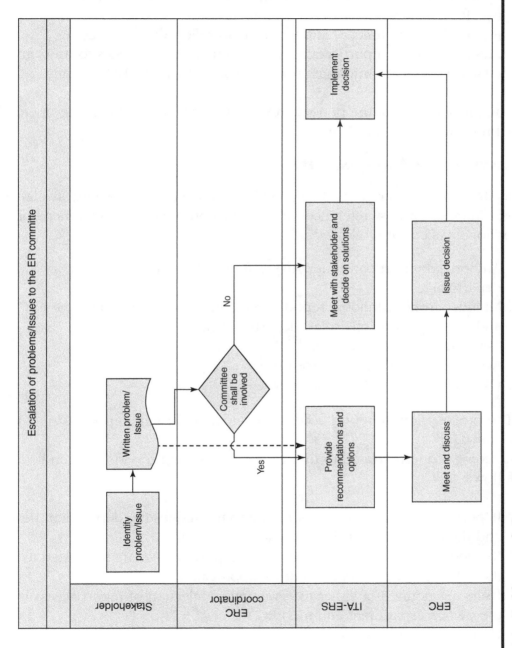

Figure 11.4   Problem escalation process.

3. ERS conducts random data validation at least once a year for all reports.
4. If data validation warrants any changes, those changes must be agreed by the owner department or the KPI owner. Changes are implemented by ERS.
5. ERS updates the functional documents to reflect any changes.
6. ERS updates the report catalog and communicates changes to users and related Healthcare Information Technology Affairs (HITA) sections.

The process flow of the periodic review and validation of existing operational reports is shown in Figure 11.5.

Reports Access Management

To facilitate access to reports, ERS produces an inventory of reports available on the intranet for easy reference. At the initiation of new report generation, the following steps are followed:

1. Authorized report consumers/users are identified by the owner department.
2. Multidepartmental/global reports access must be approved by the ERC and the requesting chairman/department head.
3. Authorized users are trained.
4. Access is granted to authorize users.
5. Users are informed of access privileges.

The process flow of report access management for new reports is shown in Figure 11.6.

Ongoing requests related to user access for existing reports are handled as follows:

1. Report access requests are submitted to the requesting department head and then to the owner department for approval.
2. Requests for multidepartmental/global reports access are submitted to the ERC and owner department for approval.
3. Users are notified of either the granting or rejection of report access by the owner department and the ERC.
4. Users are trained as necessary.

Process flow of report access management for existing reports is shown in Figure 11.7.

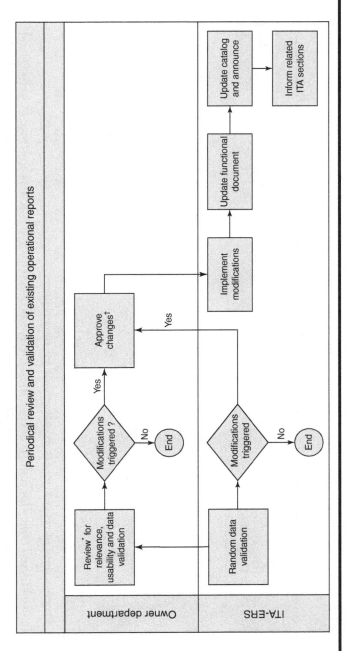

Figure 11.5 **Process flow of the review and validation of existing operational reports.**

* Periodic review of multidepartmental/global reports may require the involvement of all related stakeholders. Relevance and usability is determined by auditing the use of reports and discussing reports with their owners.
† Multidepartmental/global reports' changes require the approval of ERC, in addition to the owner department.

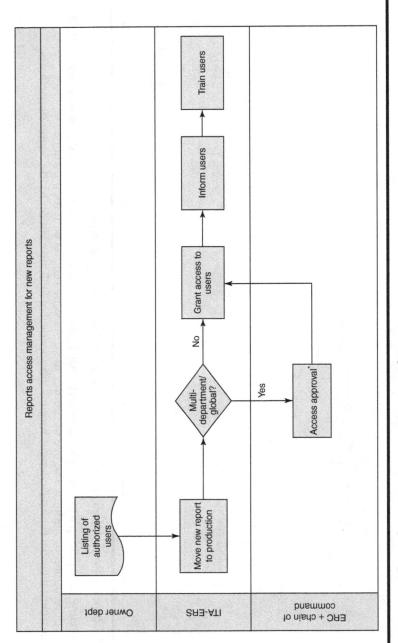

Figure 11.6 Process flow of report access management for new reports.

* If there is an established policy for reports access, then there is no need to obtain access approval from the chain of command of the relevant areas. This is particularly applicable to reports that do not require any restriction or where blanket approval is already stipulated by policy facilitated by the ERC for secretaries, head nurses, managers, etc.

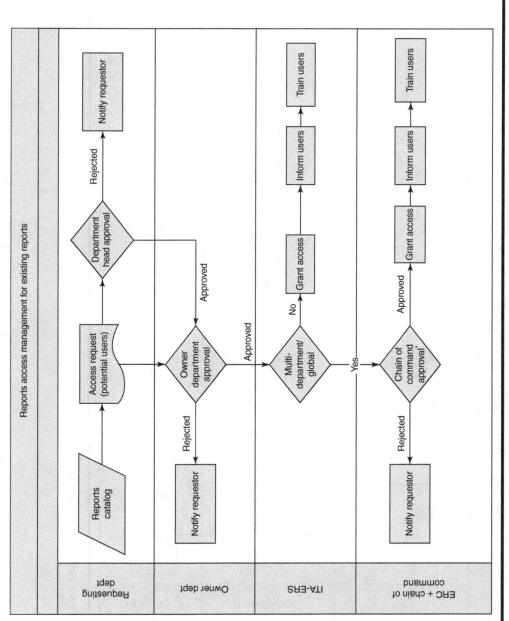

Figure 11.7   Process flow of report access management for existing reports.

* If there is an established policy for reports access, then there is no need to obtain access approval from the chain of command of the relevant areas. This is particularly relevant for reports that do not require any restriction or where blanket approval is already stipulated in policy facilitated by the ERC for secretaries, head nurses, managers, etc.

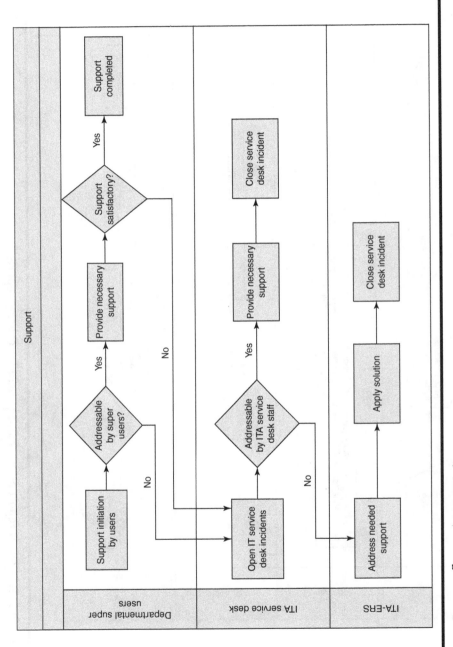

Figure 11.8 Process flow, user support.

User Support

We champion the concept of *superusers*—key users who are selected by their functional departments to receive extensive training by ERS so they have the capability to be a first line of support. These superusers are an integral part of a streamlined support process that includes the following steps:

1. Departmental superusers provide the first line of support.
2. If the support call is beyond the capability of the first line of support, then an HITA–Service Desk *incident* ticket is opened by the departmental superusers.
3. ITA Service Desk staff attend to the incident and, if it is beyond their capability, forward it to ERS for resolution.
4. ERS takes the necessary steps to resolve the incident and close it accordingly.

An HITA–Service Desk application is used for tracking and monitoring of incidents. The process flow for user support is shown in Figure 11.8.

Lessons Learned

- Defining the data warehouse report life cycle is very important.
- Appropriate stakeholders need to be involved in the validation process.
- As much as possible, problems and issues should be resolved within the working bodies before escalation.
- Access management is crucial to maintain information integrity and the need to deploy streamed processes.
- The utilization of superusers empowered with extensive training turned out to be very useful and successful.

Chapter 12

Knowledge Transfer

Fadwa Saad AlBawardi

Contents

A key component of our ongoing *knowledge management* initiative is knowledge transfer from vendors to our staff. Our goal as a modern healthcare organization is to selectively capture, archive, and access the best practices of work-related knowledge and decision making from employees, managers, and vendors. This chapter, written from the perspective of a technical team member, details our approach to managing the transfer of intellectual assets, associated with the development of our data warehouse, from vendors and consultants to our permanent staff.

Knowledge Management

We define knowledge management as a deliberate, systematic business optimization strategy that selects, distills, stores, organizes, packages, and communicates information essential to the operation of the healthcare enterprise in a manner that improves employee performance and the competitiveness of the enterprise. Knowledge management is about how to make the right knowledge available to the right people at the right time. It's also about how to best generate or acquire new relevant knowledge. The objective of knowledge management is to enhance performance as per the organization's strategic goals and objectives. Accordingly, knowledge management must therefore create or provide the proper people, resources, and tools to enhance learning and experience gaining. It must allow the creation of real value and the application of the new knowledge, as well as allow the storing of this knowledge to make it promptly available at any time to the right people. Like other modern healthcare enterprises, we cannot compete effectively in the marketplace without skilled managers and employees. Furthermore, we are dependent on their knowledge of the people, processes, and technologies involved in healthcare—especially information technology (IT).

Given our reliance on vendors for the installation and setup of imported technologies, knowledge management—and knowledge transfer in particular—is a mandatory component of our IT operations. Even though we aim to ensure vendor compliance with knowledge transfer through contractual obligations and emphasize the importance of knowledge transfer to our employees, we recognize that it is rarely complete. Professionalism comes with experience, and expertise with tools requires practice and applied problem solving. As detailed in the following section, the transfer component of our knowledge management initiative involved appropriate staffing, committing significant resources to training, and establishing a clear contractual arrangement with the vendor.

Staffing

The central staffing issue was whether to create a dedicated data warehousing development group from new hires or to borrow staff from our transaction processing development group. We chose the latter option because a separate development group would have likely lessened knowledge transfer to the entire IT department. Furthermore, the new group would not have benefited from the knowledge and experience of our transaction processing development group.

Teams

A technical project manager and a functional project manager were assigned to the data warehouse project from the start. The technical project manager acted as our single point of contact with the vendor. He facilitated and monitored all vendor interactions with our staff. The functional project manager, as the liaison between our technical team and end users, was tasked with ensuring the users' functional requirements were addressed. The technical and functional managers worked together to monitor progress, resolve issues, and track new modifications, and, in general, did what they could to enhance the project.

In addition to a dedicated technical project manager, we established knowledge transfer liaisons in our functional and technical implementation teams. Two members from our functional team were assigned to a vendor-supplied functional specialist and a consultant for the purpose of knowledge transfer. The functional team was responsible for ongoing, regular meetings held with the end users. The purpose of these meetings was to gather the necessary business information needed to formulate the KPIs used in the data warehouse.

As part of the knowledge transfer exercise, functional documents were written to reflect the user business requirements for all KPIs. This documentation, in the form of a searchable electronic repository, was the primary mechanism of transferring the KPI requirements to the technical teams in a manner that supported effective knowledge transfer. The documentation also helped the technical team understand the exact business needs and requirements of the end users as well as provided the exact functional formulas that are to be used during the technical development of the KPIs. The functional team also discussed report formats with the end users. This information was transferred to the technical team for implementation.

The functional team also had the role of a *data unit*, in that they validated and tested the report outputs for accuracy before they were delivered to executives and business users. Inaccuracies were submitted to the technical team for another cycle of revision. The quality assurance (QA) process for deliverables is essential. As such, the data unit is of great value in data validation and approval prior to submitting the deliverables to the key end users.

We established a similar knowledge transfer structure within our technical teams. Two database specialists were assigned to work with the vendor-supplied data model and erwin tool specialists, two of our extraction, transformation, and loading (ETL) specialists were paired with a vendor-supplied ETL specialist who was responsible for the Informatica tools, and three of our online analytical processing (OLAP) specialists shadowed two vendor-supplied OLAP specialists. Knowledge transfer was facilitated through joint meetings, formal training, and vendor-supplied documentation. For example, the vendor provided a five-day training session for five of our ETL and OLAP specialists to familiarize them with the data model and associated documentation. Similarly, our ETL team received formal training on KPI development.

In the future, it would be beneficial for the business intelligence (BI) technical team to have a knowledge exchange rotation between ETL and OLAP roles. This will help us build a more powerful team whose members are each aware of the complete BI process. In addition, this has proven helpful with human resources when team members must work to cover for members on planned and unplanned leave.

Verification of Transfer

As an early test of the effectiveness of knowledge transfer, we had our OLAP staff implement 10 KPIs on their own. Vendor intervention was limited to the monitoring of methodology and progress. Fortunately, our staff demonstrated competence in developing the KPIs, from obtaining basic functional documentation from the functional team to creating valid cubes, accurate analytical reports, and ReportNet reports. This exercise is necessary for achieving a successful learning curve and completing knowledge transfer.

Methodology

We used the following methods to facilitate the transfer of knowledge from the vendor to our staff.

- *Direct observation*: Our functional and technical teams observed and documented vendor activity throughout the development process, including meetings between vendor-supplied specialists and end users.

This observation was formal and with the vendor's permission. We did this daily for the duration of the project.

■ *Formal training*: Vendor-lead training sessions were held on basic data warehouse concepts, the implementation process, and the effective use of data modeling, ETL, and OLAP tools. Training is considered at length in the following section, with all details shared.

■ *Vendor documentation*: The vendor-supplied documentation in key areas, including
  − Requirement specification
  − KPI development
  − Logical data model
  − Physical data model
  − ETL design
  − Systems and integration test plan
  − End user application design
  − Data warehouse operational manual
  − End user application operational manual
  − Functional data model, ETL, and OLAP report designs
  − User acceptance testing (UAT) for final approval

  This documentation was updated and maintained by members of our functional and technical teams as we added more KPIs to the data warehouse.

■ *Practice test*: As a test of competence, we required our teams to produce 10 complete KPIs based on the information gathered by our functional team. As noted earlier, our team succeeded in developing the KPIs without assistance from the vendor. Through this and similar exercises, we were able to certify the knowledge transfer process and gain the confidence that we could implement additional KPIs without vendor supervision or intervention. After development, the KPIs were shared with the vendor for their input/feedback and final remarks on what, if anything, needed to be enhanced.

■ *Handholding*: Throughout the project, the vendor team was supportive and available to answer technical and functional questions from our staff. The vendor also helped in solving technical issues and in debugging the KPI implementations. As required by contract, the vendor also provided one year of 24/7 support following the sign-off of the implementation phase of the project.

Training

Formal, vendor-provided training was a major component of the knowledge transfer process. Full-day sessions, conducted in our facilities, included a mandatory assessment component at the end of each topic. As part of the knowledge transfer process, the vendor provided our technical staff with the transparencies and slides presented in each course. The curriculum focused on three core areas: data warehousing, databases, and hardware. The offerings are described in more detail below.

Data warehousing: Training consisted of a two-day "Quick Start" class covering an overview of data warehousing and knowledge transfer. The initial five-day advanced course covered the Cognos suite of applications available at the time—ReportNet, Power Play, Metrics Manager, Visualizer—as well as Informatica tools. The more extensive Informatica training covered the range of functionality, including how to establish connections to data sources and targets, import and create tables, gather and filter data, and process errors. Additional training was needed with each subsequent Cognos release.

Databases: As with the courses on data warehousing, the database course offerings consisted of "Quick Start" and advanced classes. The two-day "Quick Start" course provided an introduction to Oracle 9i, including relational design concepts, simple and complex query skills, and PL/SQL programming. The advanced course focused on Oracle 9i database administration. As part of the advanced course, our staff was required to configure a server using the Optimal Flexible Architecture (OFA), set up logical and physical structures, set up database and user security, add and administer users, and monitor and tune the main server areas. In addition, our staff was required to create a toolkit of administration scripts for database management and tuning.

Hardware: Following the format of the other course offering, our staff was provided with a two-day "Quick Start" course on computer hardware relevant to the data warehouse project. This was followed by a three-day advanced course that emphasized hands-on hardware installation and maintenance.

Contractual Obligations

Contractually, the vendor was required to facilitate knowledge transfer through specific documentation and training, as noted earlier. In addition, the vendor was required to fully understand the relevant online transaction processing (OLTP) data structures and to pass this understanding on to our staff through common technical workshops. Simply treating the data structures as a functional black box would have facilitated the development timetable but at the expense of knowledge transfer.

To facilitate the vendor's understanding of our in-house data structures, we provided the vendor with free access to our documentation and relevant clinical data. Because of the patient confidentiality and security issues surrounding nonclinician access to clinical data, we required the vendor to comply with strict confidentiality to the privacy rules and regulations of our institution through signing a nondisclosure agreement (NDA).

We also provided the vendor with access to test data from the source systems as required. When the vendor discovered missing or inaccurate data sources or data fields, our team addressed the gap, since this was out of scope to the vendor. Similarly, in working with source systems, the vendor integrated the data entities with the data warehouse in coordination with our technical teams. This active collaboration extended to the definition and correction of KPI formulas and benchmarks, together with the key end users, with the caveat that we reserved the right to modify formulas as necessary to suit the needs of our institution.

Vendors continue to be a source of information and education. However, our goal is to become self-sufficient as soon as possible. To this end, we view building a powerful BI team as critical to the success of our organization. For the time being, this will require additional knowledge transfer from the vendors and our team members. The BI team members covered all required roles, starting from database, ETL, data modeling, and ending with visualizations and reporting.

Lessons Learned

- The choice of an appropriate, knowledgeable, experienced, and highly professional vendor from the very beginning is crucial to the success of knowledge transfer.
- The choice of the appropriate BI tools from the start is critical to ensure compliance with industry standards and to facilitate the knowledge transfer of best practices. Several international tool assessment sites can be referenced for the selection, such as Gartner.
- Vendor team members must have excellent communication and teaching skills. Technical knowledge is not enough.

- Internal staff must be technically competent and eager to learn.
- Supervision of the knowledge transfer process is essential and should not be left to chance. Regular weekly meetings need to be conducted for progress updates from both vendors and internal staff.
- The roles and responsibilities of everyone on vendor and internal teams must be clearly defined and documented to facilitate collaboration and joint problem solving.
- Vendor plans should include sufficient time for the development, effective knowledge transfer, and training of the technical team. This will ensure that busy project timelines do not hinder the knowledge transfer at the end.
- Tacit knowledge, which is difficult to demonstrate or codify, is difficult to transfer.
- Knowledge transfer takes time. As such, team members should be given sufficient time to absorb the information and apply it themselves.
- Knowledge transfer requires a common vocabulary. Definitions of technical and functional processes should be clearly stated and documented for future reference.
- Updated/new general rules and technical adjustments throughout the project must be known to everyone in the team at all times, as well as clearly documented, for consistency.
- Documentations should always be maintained and updated in a shared, secure folder for everyone's ease of access.
- Before signing off, the reports must be 100% tested, verified, and officially accepted by the end users after UAT testing.

Epilogue

Bryan Bergeron

The story told in this book highlights many of the challenges inherent to implementing and maintaining a homegrown IT solution, from fine-tuning an RFP and working against a backdrop of a continually evolving suite of applications and IT initiatives to managing hospital politics. Given the rapid evolution in the data warehouse market, economic pressures, government incentive programs, and inevitable turnover in the vendor space, the specific solutions discussed in this book may be outdated within a few years. However, regardless of the particular technology, most, if not all, of the lessons learned during the King Faisal Specialist Hospital and Research Centre (KFSH&RC) data warehouse implementation are timeless. The core issue, after all, is people—from clinicians, patients, and vendors to administrators and programmers—not technology.

Consider the comments concerning outsourcing, most notably that key elements of successful outsourcing are to develop an effective RFP and to exercise sound vendor selection and management processes. Furthermore, outsourcing requires flexibility in approach and methods. Transparency in terms and conditions and clearly defined roles and responsibilities can be used to create a win–win relationship with the vendor. In addition, risk of failure can be minimized by a carefully crafted contract that links milestones with both incentives and penalties. These heuristics are brought to life by the experiences of the KFSH&RC management.

On the topic of staffing development teams, one clear message is that implementation is more effective if staff are available throughout the duration of a project, instead of being pulled from other projects on an ad hoc basis. Regular interaction among all members of the various implementation teams is also essential and an appropriate liaison from the functional (i.e., nontechnical) team should maintain communication with the end users. Furthermore, when an institutional goal is knowledge transfer from vendor to staff, mixed teams composed of internal and vendor personnel are viable options.

Planning is a critical component of every healthcare IT implementation. The experiences at KFSH&RC suggest that planning an outsourced implementation requires full vendor participation. Furthermore, this should begin with sharing high-level goals with prospective vendors in the RFP—not after the contract has been signed.

On the topic of knowledge transfer, the takeaways include the basics, such as assuring the competence of internal staff as well as the domain and teaching competence of vendor staff. Another basic, obvious in retrospect, is that knowledge transfer requires a common vocabulary. As such, definitions of technical and functional processes should be clearly stated and documented. In addition, supervision of the knowledge transfer process is essential and should not be left to chance. A component of supervision is clearly defining the roles and responsibilities of everyone involved in the implementation, whether internal or affiliated with the vendor. Another fundamental truism is that knowledge transfer takes time. Staff should be given sufficient time to absorb information.

Finally, and perhaps most importantly, the IT-driven implementation at KFSH&RC highlights the factors involved in achieving user buy-in. Not only is it imperative to quickly build trust in the system among the user community at the start of implementation, but outreach must continue through implementation and training. As has been demonstrated by this and countless other healthcare IT initiatives, a data warehouse or other application is simply a tool that must be trusted, accepted, and used in order to improve the quality of healthcare.

Appendix I: KPI Format

- *Name*: Average length of stay.
- *ID#*: KPI-2.01.02.
- *Short definition*: Number of days an inpatient stays in the hospital, on average, unadjusted.
- *Long definition*: According to the CDC: In the National Health Interview Survey (https://www.cdc.gov/nchs/nhis/index.htm), the average length of stay per discharged inpatient is computed by dividing the number of hospital days for a specified group by the number of discharges for that group. In the National Hospital Discharge Survey (https://www.cdc.gov/nchs/nhds/index.htm), the average length of stay is computed by dividing the number of days of care, counting the date of admission but not the date of discharge, by the number of patients discharged. The American Hospital Association (https://www.aha.org) computes the average length of stay by dividing the number of inpatient days by the number of admissions.
- *Rationale*: Average length of stay is an important indicator of hospital utilization and a metric for determining staffing requirements. When corrected for the severity of illness, it can provide a measure of hospital efficiency and effectiveness. It is also a productivity measure that is often trended and compared with benchmarks. Because the majority of hospital expenses are related to inpatient care, the current practice is to minimize the average length of stay in favor of more lucrative outpatient services. Length of stay naturally varies with the severity of illness and the patient's health.
- *Type of measure*: Outcome.
- *Improvement noted as*: A decrease in the average length of stay.

■ *Formula*: $\left[\dfrac{\text{Disharge Days}}{\text{Total Discharges}}\right]$

■ *Numerator*: Discharge days.
 - *Included population in numerator*: All inpatients included in discharge days.
 - *Excluded population in numerator*: Newborns.
 - *Data elements*:
   • Inpatient days
   • Nursing unit ID
   • Nursing division ID
   • Medical service ID
   • Physician ID
   • Medical department ID
■ *Denominator*: Discharges: Number of discharges during the reporting period.
 - *Included population in denominator*: All inpatient nursing units with admitted patients
 - *Excluded population in denominator*: Newborns
 - *Data elements*:
   • Inpatient nursing units
   • Medical departments
   • Medical department sections
   • Total discharges
■ *Data reported as*: Continuous variable measured in days.
■ *Data source*: Medical records.
■ *Data collection approach*: Retrospective.
■ *Risk adjustment*: No. Legacy formula should be used as is for benchmark purposes.
■ *Data accuracy*: Reduce manual handling of data. Certify the practice of loading data from ICIS and the mainframe doesn't introduce errors.
■ *Measure analysis suggestions*: Standard deviation should be incorporated in the outcome measure.
■ *Sampling*: Yes. However, sampling by month should be limited to non-Ramadan periods.
■ *Department/service affected*: All inpatient nursing units and all medical departments.
■ *Process affected*: This is a core metric used by the hospital management to assess the efficiency and effectiveness of staff.

■ *KPIs affected*: NA.
■ *Benchmark value(s)*:
  – *External benchmarks*
    • 5.43 days (Yale New Haven General Hospital, United States, 2014 report)
    • 5.83 days (Massachusetts General Hospital, United States, 2012 report)
    • 5.8 days (Mayo Clinic, Rochester, United States, 2010 report)
  – *Internal benchmarks*
    • 9.7 days (KFSH, 1424 YTD report)
■ *Target value*: NA.
■ *Trigger value(s)*: NA.
■ *Adjustments*: NA.
■ *Adjustment formula*: NA.
■ *Related analysis*: Trend and predictive modeling.
■ *Charting*: Control chart for primary charting.
■ *References*:
  – *KPI*: AHIMA
  – *Benchmark*: Yale New Haven Hospital: https://www.ynhh.org/about/hospitaloverview/facts-figures.aspx Massachusetts General Hospital:http://www.massgeneral.org/assets/pdf/Massachusetts%20General%20Hospital%20annual%20report_FY12.pdf Mayo Clinic:http://www.beckershospitalreview.com/lists-and-statistics/mayo-clinic-21-statistics-andfacts.html
  – *Target*: TBD
  – *Triggers*: TBD
  – *Adjustments*: NA
  – *Related analysis*: NA
  – *Charting*: *Tools for Performance Measurement in Health Care: A Quick Reference Guide*, Oakbrook Terrace, IL: Joint Commission Resources, 2008
■ *Security/privacy*: TBD.
■ *Access level*: Chief Executive Director; deputy counsel and supervisor of executive management; executive officer, medical affairs; chief operating officer; deputy chief operating officer, medical and clinical operations; assistant deputy chief operating officers, medical and clinical operations; medical department chairmen; senior administrator, medical and clinical operations; chief of nursing; deputy chief of nursing; senior administrator, clinical services; senior administrator, patient affairs;

head, case management and admissions; deputy chief operating officer, GASS; executive officer, financial affairs.

- *Acronyms and definitions*:
  - *ALOS*: Average length of stay
  - *CDC*: Centers for Disease Control (www.cdc.gov)
  - *Discharge*: A completed inpatient hospitalization for a minimum period of 24 hours
- *Owner*: Chief Operating Officer.
- *Frequency of validation*:
  - Definition: Annually
  - Benchmark: Annually
  - Trigger: Annually
  - Target: Annually
  - References: Annually

Appendix II: Information Analysis Template

Name: Average Length of Stay

Significance of KPI for Decision Making

- *Average length of stay* is an indicator of hospital utilization and metric for determining staffing requirements.
- When corrected for severity of illness, it can provide a measure of hospital efficiency and effectiveness.
- The current practice is to minimize the average length of stay in favor of more lucrative outpatient services.
- Length of stay naturally varies with severity of illness and patient health.

Report Layout

Date	Service ID	Unit ID	Discharge Days (Inpatient Days)	Total Discharges	Average Length of Stay

Purpose of report: This report will display the average length of stay.

Display of report: All date/time attributes will be displayed in DD-MMM-YY HH24:MM:SS format.

Report frequency: Monthly, quarterly, annually.

Frequency of data extraction from source system: Daily.

Drill-Down

MRN	Age	Gender	Nationality	Admission Date/Time	Discharge Date/Time	Physician ID

KPI Mapping to Source for Average Length of Stay

Business Requirement to Source System Mapping						
S. No.	Source Attributes	Source System Name/ Module Name	Source Type	Source Entity Name	KPI Data Elements	Comments/ Rules

Dimensions			
S. No.	Dimension	Associated Attribute	Description

Measure Requirements				
S. No.	Measure	Source Attributes	Formula	Description

Adjustments		
S. No.	Data Element	Adjustments

Filter Conditions		
S. No.	Name of Filter	Data Elements to Be Filtered

Gap Analysis

Required Attributes	Missing Data Elements	Remarks

Appendix III: Key Database Parameters

Database Parameter	Description
BACKGROUND_DUMP_DEST	Pathname (directory or disc) where debugging trace files for the background processes (LGWR, DBWn, and other core processes) are written during Oracle operations.
COMPATIBLE	To use a new release, while at the same time guaranteeing backward compatibility with earlier releases.
CORE_DUMP_DEST	Directory where Oracle dumps core files.
DB_BLOCK_BUFFERS	Number of database buffers in the buffer cache.
DB_BLOCK_SIZE	Size of Oracle database blocks.
DB_FILE_MULTIBLOCK_READ_COUNT	Maximum number of blocks read in one I/O operation during a sequential scan.
DB_FILES	Maximum number of database files that can be opened for this database.
DB_NAME	Database name.
DBWR_IO_SLAVES	Number of I/O server processes used by the DBW0 process. The DBW0 process and its server processes always write to disk.

(Continued)

(Continued)

Database Parameter	Description
LARGE_POOL_SIZE	Size of the large pool allocation heap. Used in multithreaded server systems for session memory, by parallel execution for message buffers, and by backup processes for disk I/O buffers.
LOG_BUFFER	Amount of memory that Oracle uses when buffering redo entries to a redo log file.
LOG_CHECKPOINT_INTERVAL	Frequency of checkpoints in terms of the number of redo log file blocks that can exist between an incremental checkpoint and the last block written to the redo log.
LOG_CHECKPOINT_TIMEOUT	Specifies that the incremental checkpoint is at the position where the last write to the redo log (sometimes called the *tail of the log*) was integer seconds ago.
MAX_ENABLED_ROLES	Maximum number of database roles that users can enable, including roles contained within other roles.
OPEN_CURSORS	Whether there are open cursors for the database link.
OPTIMIZER_MODE	Specifies the goal of optimization of SQL statements.
PARALLEL_AUTOMATIC_TUNING	Specifies whether to set parallelism feature on or off.
PGA_AGGREGRATE_TARGET	Amount of PGA memory allocated at instance level.
PROCESSES	Maximum number of operating system user processes that can simultaneously connect to Oracle. Its value should allow for all background processes such as locks, job queue processes, and parallel execution processes.

(Continued)

(Continued)

Database Parameter	Description
QUERY_REWRITE_ENABLED	Enable or disable query rewriting globally for the database.
REMOTE_LOGIN_PASSWORDFILE	Specifies whether Oracle checks for a password file and how many databases can use the password file.
SHARED_POOL_SIZE	Size of the shared pool. Shared pool contains shared cursors, stored procedures, control structures, and other structures.
STAR_TRANSFORMATION_ENABLED	Determines whether a cost-based query transformation will be applied to star queries.
TIMED_STATISTICS	Specifies whether statistics related to time are collected or not.
USER_DUMP_DEST	Pathname for a directory where the server will write debugging trace files on behalf of a user process.

Appendix IV: Physical Architecture

Server	Purpose	Configuration	Software
Informatica Production	1. Operational data store (ODS) database 2. Staging database 3. Informatica server and repository	1. Dell Power Edge R900 Series, 16 CPU Intel Xeon® 2.93 GHz with 24 GB RAM 2. Dell PowerEdge 2950 Series, 8 CPU Intel Xeon® 3.16 GHz with 16 GB RAM	Informatica 9.0.1 Services; Informatica 9.0.1 Client; MS Windows Server 2003 R2 Enterprise Edition, 32 bit; Oracle 10G Enterprise Edition
Informatica Certification	1. ODS database 2. Staging database 3. Informatica server and repository	VMware Virtual Platform, 8 CPU Intel Xeon® 2.93 GHz with 20 GB RAM	Informatica 9.0.1 Services; Informatica 9.0.1 Client; MS Windows Server 2003 R2 Enterprise Edition, 32 bit; Oracle 10G Enterprise Edition
Cognos Production	1. Generation of scorecards, dashboards analytical reporting, predictive modeling, alerts, and notifications 2. Cognos 10 repository	Dell PowerEdge R910 Series, 32 CPU Intel Xeon® 2.67 GHz with 64 GB RAM	IBM Cognos 10: • Configuration • Framework manage • Metric designer • Map manager • Transformer MS Windows Server 2008 R2 Enterprise Edition, 64 bit; Oracle 10G Enterprise Edition

(Continued)

(Continued)

Server	Purpose	Configuration	Software
Cognos Development	1. Development of scorecards, dashboards, analytical reporting, predictive modeling and forecasting, alerts, and notifications 2. Cognos repository	VMware Virtual Platform, 4 CPU Intel Xeon® 2.93 GHz with 12 GB RAM	IBM Cognos 10: • Configuration • Framework manager • Metric designer • Map manager • Transformer MS Windows Server 2008 R2 Enterprise Edition 4 bit; Oracle 10G Enterprise Edition
Data Warehouse Production	Data warehouse Production database	Dell PowerEdge R910 Series, 64 CPU Intel Xeon® 2.27 GHz with 64 GB RAM	Oracle 10G Enterprise Edition; MS Windows Server 2008 R2 Enterprise Edition, 64 bit
Data Warehouse Certification	Data Warehouse Certification database	Dell PowerEdge R900 Series, 16 CPU Intel 2.93 GHz with 24 GB RAM	Oracle 10G Enterprise Edition; MS Windows Server 2008 R2 Enterprise Edition, 64 bit
SAN Storage	1. Data Warehouse Database Files 2. Cognos Repository Database Files 3. Cognos Cube Files	Dell Compellent CT-SC40 Connectivity is FC 8 Gbps Using data progression and have two-tier storage: • Tier 1: SAS 600 GB 15 K • Tier 2: SAS 2 TB 7 K	

Appendix V: Healthcare Quality Organizations

United States

Accreditation Association for Ambulatory Health Care (AAAHC) *www.aaahc.org*

Agency for Healthcare Research and Quality (AHRQ) *www.ahrq.gov*

America's Health Insurance Plans (AHIP) *www.ahip.org*

American Association of Blood Banks (AABB) *www.aabb.org*

American Board of Medical Quality (ABMQ) *www.abmq.org*

American College of Emergency Physicians (ACEP) *www.acep.org*

American College of Surgeons (ACS) *www.facs.org*

American Dental Association (ADA) *www.ada.org*

American Health Information Management Association (AHIMA) *www.ahima.org*

American Health Quality Association (AHQA) *www.ahqa.org*

American Hospital Association (AHA) *www.aha.org*

American Medical Association (AMA) *www.ama-assn.org*

American Nurses Association (ANA) *www.ana.org*

American Optometric Association (AOA) *www.aoa.org*

American Organization of Nurse Executives (AONE) *www.aone.org*

American Osteopathic Association (AOA) *www.aoa-net.org*

American Pharmacists Association (APhA) *www.aphanet.org*

American Society for Healthcare Risk Management (ASHRM) *www.ashrm.org*

American Society for Quality (ASQ) *www.asq.org*

American Society of Health-System Pharmacists (ASHP) *www.ashp.org*

American Society of Histocompatibility and Immunogenetics (ASHI) *www.ashi-hla.org*

Anesthesia Patient Safety Foundation (APSF) *www.apsf.org*
Association of American Medical Colleges (AAMC) *www.aamc.org*
Automotive Industry Action Group (AIAG) *www.aiag.org*
Aviation Safety Reporting System (ASRS) *asrs.arc.nasa.gov*
Baldrige Performance Excellence Program (BPEP) *www.nist.gov/baldrige*
Care Quality Commission (CQC) *www.cqc.com*
Centers for Disease Control (CDC) *www.cdc.gov*
CDC Division of Healthcare Quality Promotion (DHQP) *www.cdc.gov/ncezid/dhqp*
CDC Healthcare-Associated Infections *www.cdc.gov/hai*
Center for Information Technology Leadership (CITL) *www.citl.org*
Centers for Medicare & Medicaid Services (CMS) *www.cms.hhs.gov*
COLA *www.cola.org*
College of American Pathologists (CAP) *www.cap.org*
Food and Drug Administration (FDA) *www.fda.gov*
Hospital and Health System Association of Pennsylvania *www.haponline.org*
Institute for Healthcare Improvement *www.ihi.org*
Institute for Safe Medication Practices *www.ismp.org*
Joint Commission International (JCI) *www.jointcommission.org*
Joint Commission on Accreditation of Healthcare Organizations (JCAHO) *www.jcaho.org*
Kaiser Permanente *www.kaiserpermanente.org*
Leapfrog Group *www.leapfroggroup.org*
Medical Group Management Association *www.mgma.com*
National Academy for State Health Policy *www.nashp.org*
National Association for Healthcare Quality *www.nahq.org*
National Association of Chain Drug Stores *www.nacds.org*
National Coalition on Health Care *www.nchc.org*
National Committee for Quality Assurance (NCQA) *www.ncqa.org*
National Coordinating Council on Medication Error Reporting and Prevention (NCCMERP) *www.nccmerp.org*
National Quality Forum (NQF) *www.qualityforum.org*
National Health Policy Forum (NHPF) *www.nhpf.org*
National Patient Safety Foundation *www.npsf.org*
Partnership for Patient Safety *www.p4ps.org*
Pharmaceutical Research and Manufacturers of America (PhRMA) *www.phrma.org*
U.S. Department of Veterans Affairs (VA) *www.va.gov*
U.S. Pharmacopeial Convention (USP) *www.usp.org*

Australia

Australian Association for Quality Health Care (AAQHC) *www.aaqhc.org.au*
Australian Commission on Safety and Quality in Health Care *www.safety-andquality.gov.au*
Australian Council on Healthcare Standards (ACHS) *www.achs.org.au*
Australian Healthcare and Hospitals Association (AHHA) *www.ahha.asn.au*
Australian Patient Safety Foundation (APSF) *www.apsf.net.au*

Canada

Accreditation Canada *www.accreditation.ca*
Standards Council of Canada (SCC) *www.scc.ca*

International

International Organization for Standardization (ISO) *www.iso.org*

United Kingdom

National Health Service (NHS) *www.nhs.uk*
QHA Trent Accreditation *www.qha-trent.co.uk*
UK Akkreditering Forum Limited (UKAF) *www.ukaf.org.uk*

Appendix VI: Departmental KPI Wish List

KPI	Department
OR utilization	OR/Anesthesia
OR turnaround time	OR/Anesthesia
OR cancellation rate	OR/Anesthesia
Number of anesthesia hours per anesthetist	OR/Anesthesia
Time taken per procedure per specialty	OR/Anesthesia
Number of cases per specialty per physician per day	OR/Anesthesia
Procedure starting delay time	OR/Anesthesia
Inventory utilization rate	OR/Anesthesia
Percentage of overtime	Nursing
Variance NAPPI (Non-Adverse Psychological and Physical Interventions)	Nursing
Percentage of sick time	Nursing
Percentage of pressure ulcers	Nursing
Staff turnover rate (%)	Nursing
Percentage of staff in zones 1, 2, and 4	Nursing
Percentage of fall incidents	Nursing
Central line infection rates	Nursing
Ventilator-associated pneumonias	Nursing
Urinary catheter infection rates	Nursing

(Continued)

(Continued)

KPI	Department
Surgical mortality rate	Nursing
Admissions/discharges/transfers	Nursing
Clinical education hours per nurse	Nursing
Number of expired nurse licenses	Nursing
Number of beds open per unit	Nursing
Occupancy rate	Nursing
Current unit census	Nursing
Number of staff per unit	Nursing
Number of sick calls	Nursing
Percentage of SNI (Student Nurse Internship) sick	Nursing
Number of OT patients	Nursing
Number of admits	Nursing
Number of transfers in	Nursing
Number of transfers out	Nursing
Number of discharges	Nursing
Maximum number of open beds available	Nursing
Beds open above safe staffing level	Nursing
SNI budgeted lines	Nursing
SNI lines filled	Nursing
SNI percent vacancy	Nursing
Percentage of SNI leave	Nursing
Percentage of SNI available	Nursing
SNI required as per current census	Nursing
Lab inpatient utilization rate	CSD
Lab outpatient utilization rate	CSD
Radiology inpatient utilization rate	CSD
Radiology outpatient utilization rate	CSD

(Continued)

(Continued)

KPI	Department
Pharmacy inpatient utilization rate	CSD
Pharmacy outpatient utilization rate	CSD
Reported medication dispensing errors	CSD
Reported lab specimen adverse occurrence	CSD
Average waiting time for OPD CT	CSD
Average waiting time for OPD MRI	CSD
Average waiting time for OPD Neurophysiology	CSD
Percentage of OPD pharmacy wait times <20 minutes	CSD
Percentage of OPD specimens collected <20 minutes	CSD
Number of pharmaceuticals unavailable per day	CSD
Percentage of scheduled PM completed	CSD
Staff satisfaction (biannual)	CSD
Vacancy rate	CSD
Staff turnover rate	CSD
Percentage of budget variance—Chapter 1	CSD
Percentage of budget variance—Chapter 2 (201, 202, 203)	CSD
Percentage of overtime hours (3)	CSD
Percentage of sick leave hours (4)	CSD
Percentage of targeted positions Saudized	CSD
Paid hours/adjusted patient days	CSD
Pharmaceutical expenses/adjusted patient days	CSD
Average number of CE hours per professional staff (SCHS – Saudi Commission for Health Services)	CSD
Percentage of staff compliant with life support training requirements	CSD
Percentage of staff trained in customer service	CSD
Percentage of staff trained in PI (Primary Investigator) training module	CSD

(Continued)

(Continued)

KPI	Department
Percentage of staff trained in fire safety	CSD
CS (Clinical Services) inpatient satisfaction	CSD
CS outpatient satisfaction	CSD
Number of new charts opened	MCO
ED waiting time	MCO
ALOS	MCO
Bed occupancy rate	MCO
OR cancellation rate	MCO
Percentage of day case surgeries	MCO
Number of delinquent medical records	MCO
Mortality rate	MCO
Surgical mortality rate	MCO
Return to critical care (unexpected)	MCO
Readmission through ED within 7 days of discharge	MCO
Average turnaround time for reporting results—X-rays	MCO
Average turnaround time for reporting results—CT	MCO
Average turnaround time for reporting results—MRI	MCO
Paid hours/adjusted patient day	MCO
Percentage of overtime of total worked hours	MCO
Rate of pharmaceutical failure requests	MCO
Surgical mortality rate	MCO
Ventilator-associated pneumonia rate	MCO
Central line infection rate	MCO
Urinary catheter–associated tract infection rate	MCO
Percentage of overtime of total worked hours	MCO
CABG (Coronary Artery Bypass Surgery) wound infection rate	MCO
Number of new patients accepted	MCO

(Continued)

(Continued)

KPI	Department
Number of patients rejected due to capacity	MCO
Number of day surgery procedures	MCO
Rate of pharmaceutical request failures	MCO
ICIS downtime hours	MCO
Number of medication errors reported	MCO
Number of adverse occurrences reported	MCO
Number of employees	MCO
Attrition rate	MCO
Operation expense/adjusted patient day	MCO
Accounts payable >40 days (million SR)	MCO
Accounts payable <40 days (million SR)	MCO
Number of new publications—medical	MCO
Number of clinics with wait time of >1 month	MCO
Number of patients with LOS >20 days	MCO
Number of patients admitted	MCO
Number of OR cases	MCO
OR utilization rate	MCO
Outpatient clinic visits	MCO
Number of FTEs per bed	MCO
Employee turnover rate	MCO
Manpower expense/adjusted patient day	MCO
Average CME hours provided per department (SCHS)	MCO
Average CME hours obtained per consultant (SCHS)	MCO
FTEs adjusted per patient day	MCO
TAT for a specific test/procedure or a group of tests/ procedures within a given time frame by subsection/section	Pathology
Real TAT for specific tests/procedure or group of tests/ procedures by bench/instrument	Pathology

(Continued)

(Continued)

KPI	Department
TAT for tests/procedures along with a number of procedures per hour at each bench/instrument, over a specified period of time	Pathology
Real-time patient waiting time in specimen collection areas throughout the hospital	Pathology
TAT and number of tests/procedures verified by technologist over a specified period of time by bench/instrument	Pathology
Number of tests/procedures performed by section and by the department over a specified period of time	Pathology
Number of a specific test/procedure performed over a specified period of time by subsection/section	Pathology
Number of specific tests/procedures and frequency of ordering the same tests/procedures for each patient by a specific physician	Pathology
Cost of supplies and reagents by section, monthly and yearly; information layered with number of tests/ procedures generated by each section	Pathology
Extraction of patient results in a customized format on demand based on service needs and research requirements	Pathology
Monthly and yearly monitoring of staffing budget cost code/ section budget for the merit increase and average number of steps given by cost code and by department	Pathology
Monthly and yearly monitoring of overtime budget by cost code/section and for the department	Pathology
Monthly and yearly monitoring of the number of staff for each cost code by zone mix and associated monthly and yearly	Pathology
Cost/budget. Information to be overlaid with the number of tests/procedures produced by each cost code along with TAT for a specific group of tests.	Pathology
Breakdown of TAT to basic components: active collection, collection received, received analysis, analysis verified	Pathology
Number of collected accessions performed by phlebotomist, by station and by section over a specified period of time	Pathology

(Continued)

(Continued)

KPI	*Department*
Number of collected containers performed by phlebotomist, by station and by section over a specified period of time	Pathology
Number of received containers performed by individual, by login station and by section over a specified period of time	Pathology
Total of each blood product type transfused—e.g., platelets, etc.	Blood Bank
Total of each blood product type that is wasted	Blood Bank
Number of blood product modifications that is filtered, irradiated	Blood Bank
Number of donations—e.g., plateletpheresis	Blood Bank
Total of components made from each blood donation	Blood Bank
Number of donors in age range broken down by nationality	Blood Bank
Number of blood units available in the inventory	Blood Bank
Length of stay in MSICU West and East stratified to admitting services	Critical Care (MSICU)
ICU mortality in MSICU West and East stratified to admitting services	Critical Care (MSICU)
Bed occupancy in MSICU West and East, respectively	Critical Care (MSICU)
Number of patients with unscheduled readmission within 48 hours of discharge	Critical Care (MSICU)
Number of ventilator days	Critical Care (MSICU)
Number of central line days	Critical Care (MSICU)
Number of indwelling urinary catheter days	Critical Care (MSICU)
Number of OR cases cancelled due lack of beds in ICU	Critical Care (MSICU)
Severity of illness using APACHE III score as benchmark for predicted mortality (part of Cerner's I-Net application) as per admitting primary service	Critical Care (MSICU)

(Continued)

(Continued)

KPI	Department
Mean age of patients admitted to MSICU West and East (and for each admitting services)	Critical Care (MSICU)
Gender mix of patients admitted to MSICU West and East (and from each admitting service)	Critical Care (MSICU)
Number of patients admitted to MSICU West and East, respectively	Critical Care (MSICU)
Number of patients admitted to MSICU West and East, stratified to weekday of admission, time of admission, and primary services	Critical Care (MSICU)
Admissions as per administrative order with MRNs (Medical Record Numbers) listed	Critical Care (MSICU)
Admissions directly from OR (scheduled or nonscheduled)	Critical Care (MSICU)
Admissions from regular wards	Critical Care (MSICU)
Admissions from emergency	Critical Care (MSICU)
Admissions from outside hospitals (medevac or ambulance transfers)	Critical Care (MSICU)
Number of patient days	Critical Care (MSICU)
ICU mortality in MSICU West and East, respectively	Critical Care (MSICU)
Length of stay in MSICU West and East, respectively	Critical Care (MSICU)
Hospital mortality for patients admitted to MSICU West and East	Critical Care (MSICU)
Hospital mortality for patients admitted to MSICU stratified to admitting services	Critical Care (MSICU)
Number of patients transferred to regular wards, other ICUs within KFSH&RC, other healthcare facilities, or directly home	Critical Care (MSICU)

(Continued)

(Continued)

KPI	*Department*
Number of discharged patients fulfilling ICU D/C criteria	Critical Care (MSICU)
Number of patients discharged with ICU D/C criteria waived by physician following triage	Critical Care (MSICU)
Number of patients where ICU D/C criteria were not applicable due to transfer to other monitored area	Critical Care (MSICU)
Number of patients where transfer from ICU delayed (h) due to lack of floor bed	Critical Care (MSICU)
Number of patients admitted as per listed admission criteria (diagnostic and objective)	Critical Care (MSICU)
Number of patients on mechanical ventilation	Critical Care (MSICU)
Mean duration of mechanical ventilation as per admitting service	Critical Care (MSICU)
Number of devices used during ICU stay (as per specified list)	Critical Care (MSICU)
Number of events where CPR was performed	Critical Care (MSICU)
Number of patients placed on "No CPR" in MSICU	Critical Care (MSICU)
Number of patients admitted with "No CPR" order in place	Critical Care (MSICU)
Number of patients where brain death was diagnosed	Critical Care (MSICU)
Number of patients where organ donation was refused by relatives	Critical Care (MSICU)
Number of patients where organ donation not performed (as per SCOT [Saudi Center for Organ Transfer] decision)	Critical Care (MSICU)
Number of brain-dead patients where organ donation was performed	Critical Care (MSICU)
Sequential organ failure score (SOFA) as per admitting primary service	Critical Care (MSICU)

(*Continued*)

(Continued)

KPI	Department
Number of ICU procedures performed (as per specified list)	Critical Care (MSICU)
Utilization of special therapies and monitoring (as per specified list)	Critical Care (MSICU)
ICU complications as per organ systems (as per listed code number)	Critical Care (MSICU)
Radiology contribution to length of stay	Radiology
Total procedures performed	Radiology
Total procedures performed per section	Radiology
Total procedures performed per priority	Radiology
Number of procedures performed per patient day	Radiology
Number of procedures performed per admission	Radiology
Number of procedures performed per patient type	Radiology
Overtime utilization as percentage of total staff payment	Radiology
Locum contract cost as percentage of total staff payment	Radiology
FTEs per procedure	Radiology
FTEs per weighted procedure (when including exam complexity)	Radiology
Outcome analysis—report accuracy	Radiology
Number of research activities undertaken by radiology staff	Radiology
Number of CMEs achieved by radiology staff	Radiology
Productivity based on total available staffing hours	Radiology
Productivity based on payroll	Radiology
Productivity based on personnel	Radiology
Productivity based on relative unit per procedure	Radiology
Productivity based on technical components	Radiology
Productivity based on professional components	Radiology
Number of procedures completed	Radiology
Total cost of a procedure	Radiology

(Continued)

(Continued)

KPI	Department
Weighed output adjusted against test complexity/procedure	Radiology
Waiting time for procedure (time of request for examination to time of actual appointment)	Radiology
Waiting time between entry of request and performance of examination	Radiology
Report turnaround time	Radiology
Time taken between dictation and verification of radiology report	Radiology
Total revenue generated by Radiology department	Radiology
Revenue generated by patient category (IPD and OPD)	Finance
Manpower expenses—payroll	Finance
Supplies expenses	Finance
Contracts expenses	Finance
Project expenses	Finance
Revenue generated by department/physician	Finance
Revenue collected (account receivable)	Finance
Manpower expenses by department	Finance
Expenses by department cost centers and accounts	Finance
Current assets	Finance
Current liabilities	Finance
Hospital grant revenue—department	Finance
Hospital grant revenue—research	Finance
Hospital grant expense by department	Finance
Hospital grant expense by research grant	Finance
Evening private clinic—Revenue collected	Finance
Evening private clinic—Expenses	Finance
Evening private clinic—Revenue per specialty	Finance
Evening private clinic—Revenue by service type	Finance

(*Continued*)

(Continued)

KPI	Department
Outstanding payable by vendor	Finance
Contract revenue by provider	Finance
Cash balance	Finance
Cost of services	Finance
Net profit by department	Finance
Net profit—organization	Finance
Family visit by ID	Finance
Sick leave—unit-wise and department-wise	Finance
Overtime bonus	Finance
Overtime expenses	Finance
Employee liability	Finance
Percentage of overtime expenses linked with sick leave	Finance
Number of patients in the scheduled appointment list per service	Medicine
Number of patients in the admissions waiting list per service	Medicine
Number of patients that are emergencies/in urgent clinics/scheduled/transferred	Medicine
Inpatient census per service	Medicine
Occupancy rate per service	Medicine
Average length of stay per service	Medicine
Corrected length of stay (patients staying less than 30 days)	Medicine
Longest stay patients	Medicine
Number of patients staying longer than 30 days	Medicine
Number of patients eligible for admission	Eligibility section (Medical Affairs)
Time from acceptance till time of first appointment	Eligibility section (Medical Affairs)
Number of transfers of eligible patients between medical devices	Eligibility section (Medical Affairs)

(*Continued*)

(Continued)

KPI	Department
Number of new referrals to palliative care	Oncology
Number of follow-ups in palliative care OPD	Oncology
New inpatient referrals for palliative care consultation	Oncology
Length of stay in Tertiary Palliative Care Unit	Oncology
Total palliative care referrals to home healthcare service	Oncology
Survival rate stage by stage for different cancer sites compared to published international data	Oncology
Number of cancer patients seen at KFCC (internal and external referrals)	Oncology
Workload per consultant per service at KFCC	Oncology
Time taken from acceptance of patient until receipt of active treatment	Oncology
Number of files submitted per physician/nurse/technical staff monthly/annually	HR/Personnel
Number of filled position per physician/nurse/technical staff monthly/annually	HR/Personnel
Number of approved positions physician/nurse/technical staff monthly/annually	HR/Personnel
Number of withdrawn candidates physician/nurse/technical staff monthly/annually	HR/Personnel
Number of files under review physician/nurse/technical staff monthly/annually	HR/Personnel
Number of rejected files physician/nurse/technical staff monthly/annually	HR/Personnel
Number of vacant positions physician/nurse/technical staff monthly/annually	HR/Personnel
Number of locum positions filled in per month	HR/Personnel
Staff turnover rate per physician/nurse/technician	HR/Personnel
Number of Western staff hired per month	HR/Personnel
Number of Saudi candidates recruited per month/annually	HR/Personnel

(*Continued*)

(Continued)

KPI	Department
Number of staff as per nationality	HR/Personnel
Number of new hired employees given sign-on bonus per zone	HR/Personnel
Number of contracted agencies	HR/Personnel
Number of requests received	Logistics
Number of POs issued/issued within 30 days	Logistics
Number of requests with no PO	Logistics
Total value of POs issued	Logistics
Number of outstanding and overdue POs plus value	Logistics
Number of POs received	Logistics
Number of line items received	Logistics
Number of items pending in receiving	Logistics
Number of items rejected	Logistics
Value of items received	Logistics
Number of items requested in warehouses	Logistics
Number of items shipped	Logistics
Number of zero-stock items	Logistics
Total value of items requested	Logistics
Total value of items shipped	Logistics
Total value of drugs issued to pharmacy compared to value of drugs dispensed to patients	Logistics
Value of medical disposable items issued to certain cost centers compared to the number of procedures done	Logistics
Number of ventilator days	Critical Care (PICU)
Number of central line days	Critical Care (PICU)
Number of indwelling urinary catheter days	Critical Care (PICU)
Number of central line–associated infections	Critical Care (PICU)
Number of ventilator-associated pneumonias	Critical Care (PICU)

(Continued)

(Continued)

KPI	Department
Number of indwelling urinary catheter–associated urinary tract infections	Critical Care (PICU)
Number of spontaneous accidental intubations	Critical Care (PICU)
Number of inpatient days	Critical Care (PICU)
PICU mortality rate	Critical Care (PICU)
Number of unscheduled returns to ICU	Critical Care (PICU)
Mortality rate categorized by specified DRG	Critical Care (PICU)
Number of inpatient discharges categorized by specified DRGs	Critical Care (PICU)
Number of transfers out of ICU	Critical Care (PICU)
Number of physical restraint days	Critical Care (PICU)
Number of patients experiencing one or more physical restraint events	Critical Care (PICU)
Number of sedation and analgesia episodes with recorded oxygen saturation	Critical Care (PICU)
Number of sedation and analgesia episodes with recorded mild oxygen saturation	Critical Care (PICU)
Number of sedation and analgesia episodes with recorded severe oxygen saturation	Critical Care (PICU)
Number of sedation and analgesia episodes where airway obstruction occurred	Critical Care (PICU)
Number of sedation and analgesia episodes where a drop in systolic blood pressure >20% occurred	Critical Care (PICU)
Number of spontaneous accidental tracheostomy dislodgement	Critical Care (PICU)
Number of times required therapy is not available	Critical Care (PICU)
Monthly average CME hours per consultant per department	Academic and Training Affairs
Room booking occupancy rate	Academic and Training Affairs

(*Continued*)

(Continued)

KPI	Department
Enrollments per program per resident/fellow/short-term trainees/medical scholars	Academic and Training Affairs
Completions per program for a given period per resident/fellow/short-term trainee	Academic and Training Affairs
End of trainee count per program per training level per resident/fellow	Academic and Training Affairs
Expected completions per program for a given period per resident/fellow	Academic and Training Affairs
Number of stock items in warehouse	Academic and Training Affairs
Number of patients with coronary artery disease	Cardiology
Number of patients with coronary artery disease associated with	Cardiology
1. Valve disease—rheumatic and non-rheumatic	Cardiology
2. Adult congenital disease	Cardiology
3. Congenital disease	Cardiology
Cardiology department mortality rates	Cardiology
Cardiology department patient acceptance rate (eligibility)	Cardiology
Occupancy rate	Cardiology
ALOS	Cardiology
Number of patient transfers	Cardiology
Inventory utilization rate	Cardiology

Acronyms

A&E	Accident and Emergency Department
AABB	American Association of Blood Banks
AAMC	Association of American Medical Colleges
AAPCC	adjusted average per capita cost
AAQHD	Australian Association for Quality Health Care
ABMS	American Board of Medical Specialties
ACA	Affordable Care Act/Allowance for Contractual Adjustments
ACC	American College of Cardiology
ACHS	Australian Council on Health Standards
ACR	American College of Radiology
ACRRVS	American College of Radiology Relative Value Scale
AD	active directory
ADA	allowance for doubtful accounts
ADE	adverse drug event
ADL	activity of daily living
ADT	admission–discharge–transfer
AERS	adverse event reporting system
AES	Advanced Encryption Standard
AFS	Administrative and Financial Services
AHA	American Hospital Association
AHCPR	Agency for Health Care Policy and Research (now AHRQ)
AHIMA	American Health Information Management Association
AHRQ	Agency for Healthcare Research and Quality
AI	artificial intelligence
AIDS	Acquired Immune Deficiency Syndrome
ALOS	average length of service/average length of stay
AMA	American Medical Association
AMAP	American Medical Accreditation Program

ANCC	American Nurses Credentialing Center
ANSI	American National Standards Institute
AOA	American Optometric Association
AONE	American Organization of Nurse Executives
APA	American Pharmaceutical Association
APC	Ambulatory Payment Classification
APSF	Anesthesia Patient Safety Foundation
ARRA	American Recover and Reinvestment Act
ASHI	American Society of Histocompatibility and Immunogenetics
ASHP	American Society of Health-System Pharmacists
ASHRM	American Society for Healthcare Risk Management
ASPE	Assistant Secretary for Planning and Evaluation
ASQ	American Society for Quality
ASRS	Aviation Safety Reporting System
ASTM	American Society for Testing and Materials
ATA	Academic and Training Affairs
BBA	Balanced Budget Act
BBRA	Balanced Budget Refinement Act
BI	business intelligence
BIPA	Benefits Improvement and Protection Act
BNQP	Baldrige National Quality Program
BPM	business performance management
BRFSS	Behavioral Risk Factor Surveillance System
BSC	balanced score card
BSI	British Standards Institution
CAD	computer-aided dispatch
CAHMI	Child and Adolescent Health Measurement Initiative
CAHPS	Consumer Assessment of Health Plans Study
CAM	complementary or alternative medicine
CAMHS	child and adolescent mental health services
CAP	College of American Pathologists
CC	comorbidity or complication
CDC	Centers for Disease Control and Prevention
CDCTB	National Tuberculosis Surveillance System
CE	continuing education
CEO	chief executive officer
CERT	Centers for Education and Research in Therapeutics
CFO	chief financial officer
CHI	Commission for Health Improvement

CHIN	Community Health Information Network
CHIPS	Center for Health Information Performance
CLIA	Clinical Laboratory Improvement Amendments
CMC	correctional managed care
CME	continuing medical education
CMI	case mix index
CMR	case management record
CMS	Centers for Medicare and Medicaid Services
CNST	Clinical Negligence Scheme for Trusts
COB	coordination of benefits
COGS	cost of goods sold
COO	chief operating officer
COPD	chronic obstructive pulmonary disease
COPPA	Children's Online Privacy Protection Act
CPM	clinical performance measure
CPO	chief privacy officer
CPOE	computerized physician order entry
CPT	current procedural terminology
CSA	Canadian Standards Association
CSFII	Continuing Survey of Food Intake by Individuals
CSHCN	children with special health care needs
CSICU	Cardiac Surgery Intensive Care Unit
CTV	composite time value
CY	calendar year
DBA	database administrator
DFC	Dialysis Facility Compare
DFR	direct financial reward
DHCP	Dynamic Host Configuration Protocol
DHHS	Department of Health and Human Services
DHQP	Division of Healthcare Quality Promotion
DICOM	Digital Imaging and Communications in Medicine
DM	disease management
DMO	Dental Maintenance Organization
DON	Diabetes Outreach Network
DPR	drug peer review
DPU	distinct part unit
DRG	diagnosis-related group
DSM-IV	Diagnostic and Statistical Manual of Mental Disorders, 4th Edition

DSS	decision support system
DTC	direct to consumer
DWV	dental weighted value
EBIT	earnings before interest and taxes
EBITAR	earnings before interest, taxes, and rent
ECHO	Experience of Care and Health Outcomes Survey (HEDIS)
ECRI	Emergency Care Research Institute
ED	Emergency Department
EDI	electronic data interchange
EMR	electronic medical record
EMV	expected money value
EOC	episode of care
EPAD	expenses per adjusted discharge
EPAPD	expenses per adjusted patient day
EPM	enterprise performance management
ER	Emergency Room
ERISA	Employee Retirement Income Security Act
ERM	employee relationship management
ERP	enterprise resource planning
ETL	extraction, transformation, and loading
EVA	economic value added
FAA	Federal Aviation Administration
FACCT	Foundation for Accountability
FAP	facility admission profile
FDA	Food and Drug Administration
FDASIA	Food and Drug Administration Safety and Innovation Act
FERPA	Family Educational Rights and Privacy Act
FHA	Federal Health Architecture
FIFO	first in, first out
FMG	Facility Management Group
FSA	flexible spending account
FTE	full-time equivalent
GAAP	generally accepted accounting principles
GAF	global assessment of functioning
GCC	Gulf Cooperation Council
GDP	gross domestic product
GLB	Gramm–Leach–Bliley Act
GME	graduate medical education
GP	general practitioner

HCFA	Health Care Financing Administration (now CMS)
HCPCS	Healthcare Common Procedure Coding System
HCSUS	HIV Cost and Services Utilization Study
HCUP	Healthcare Cost and Utilization Project
HEDIS	Health Plan and Employer Data Information Set
HES	hospital episode statistics
HHA	Home Health Agency
HHQI	Home Health Quality Initiative
HHS	Health and Human Services
HIC	Health Information Committee
HIM	health information management
HIMA	Health Industry Manufacturers Association
HIP	hospital insurance program
HIPAA	Healthcare Insurance Portability and Accountability Act
HIS	hospital information system
HITECH	Health Information Technology for Economic and Clinical Health Act
HL7	Health Level 7
HMO	health maintenance organization
HNA	health needs assessment
HOPPS	Hospital Outpatient Prospective Payment System
HRSA	Health Resources and Services Administration
HSA	health savings account
HSR&D	Health Services Research and Development Service
I/O	input/output
ICD-10	International Classification of Diseases, 10th Revision
ICD-10-AM	International Statistical Classification of Diseases and Related Health Problems, 10th Revision, Australian Modification
ICD-9-CM	International Classification of Diseases, 9th Revision, with Clinical Modifications
ICIS	Integrated Clinical Information System
ICS	International Classification for Standards
ICU	Intensive Care Unit
IDS	integrated delivery system
IHI	Institute for Healthcare Improvement
IIHI	individually identifiable health information
IMS	indicator measurement system
IOM	Institute of Medicine
IPA	Independent Practice Association

IPD	Inpatient Department
IQA	Institute of Quality Assurance
IQI	inpatient quality indicator
IRR	internal rate of return
ISMP	Institute for Safe Medication Practices
ISO	International Organization for Standardization
IT	information technology
ITA	Information Technology Affairs
IWA	International Workshop Agreement
JCAHO	Joint Commission for Accreditation of Healthcare Organization
JCI	Joint Commission International
JCIA	Joint Commission on International Accreditation
JIT	just-in-time
KFCC	King Faisal Cancer Centre
KFHI	King Faisal Heart Institute
KFSH&RC	King Faisal Specialist Hospital and Research Centre
KPI	key performance indicator
KPS	Karnofsky performance score
LDM	logical data model
LGWR	Log Writer (Component of Oracle Database Engine)
LHI	leading health indicator
LIFO	last in, first out
LMWH	low-molecular-weight heparin
LOINC	Logical Observation Identifiers Names and Codes
LOS	length of stay
LTC	long-term care
M&M	morbidity and mortality
MADS	maximum annual debt service
MAR	medical administration record
MBHO	managed behavioral healthcare organization
MBO	management by objective
MCI	medical and clinical informatics
MCO	managed care organization/medical and clinical operations
MDS	minimum data set
MEC	Medical Executive Committee
MEPS	medical expenditure panel survey
MER	medical error reporting
MERS-TM	Medical Event-Reporting System for Transfusion Medicine
MPSMS	Medicare Patient Safety Monitoring System

MQMS	Medicare Quality Monitoring System
MRI	magnetic resonance imaging
MRP	material requirements planning
MS SQL	Microsoft Standard Query Language
MSICU	Medical/Surgical Intensive Care Unit
MSO	Management Service Organization
MTBF	mean time before failure
MTF	Monitoring the Future
NAEPP	National Asthma Education and Prevention Program
NAMCS	National Ambulatory Medical Care Survey
NASA	National Aeronautics and Space Administration
NCBD	National CAHPS Benchmarking Database
NCC-MERP	National Coordinating Council for Medication Error Reporting and Prevention
NCI	National Cancer Institute
NCPIE	National Council on Patient Information and Education
NCQA	National Committee for Quality Assurance
NEMA	National Equipment Manufacturers Association
NETSS	National Electronic Telecommunications System for Surveillance
NHA	National Health Accounts
NHAMCS	National Hospital Ambulatory Medical Care Survey
NHANES	National Health and Nutrition Examination Survey
NHDR	National Healthcare Disparities Report
NHDS	National Hospital Discharge Survey
NHHCS	National Home Health and Hospice Care Survey
NHIS	National Health Interview Survey
NHPF	National Health Policy Forum
NHPPD	nursing hours per patient day
NHQR	National Healthcare Quality Report
NHS	National Health Service
NHSDA	National Household Survey on Drug Abuse
NICU	Neonatal Intensive Care Unit
NIDDK	National Institute of Diabetes and Digestive and Kidney Diseases
NIH	National Institutes of Health
NIOSH	National Institute for Occupational Safety and Health
NIS	National Immunization Survey
NIST	National Institutes of Standards and Technology

NKF	National Kidney Foundation
NLHI	National Library of Healthcare Indicators
NNDSS	National Notifiable Disease Surveillance System
NNHS	National Nursing Home Survey
NNIS	National Nosocomial Infections Surveillance
NORA	National Occupational Research Agenda
NPLHD	National Profile of Local Health Departments
NPSF	National Patient Safety Foundation
NPV	net present value
NQF	National Quality Forum
NSFG	National Survey of Family Growth
NTBSS	National TB Surveillance System
NTSB	National Transportation Safety Board
NVSS	National Vital Statistics System
NVSS-I	National Vital Statistics System: Linked Birth and Infant Death Data
NVSS-M	National Vital Statistics System: Mortality
NVSS-N	National Vital Statistics System: Natality
NwHIN	Nationwide Health Information Network
NWHPS	National Worksite Health Promotion Survey
OASIS	Outcome and Assessment Information Set
OBQI	outcome-based quality improvement
OBRA	Omnibus Budget Reconciliation Act
ODS	operational data store
OECD	Organization for Economic Cooperation and Development
OFA	Optimal Flexible Architecture
OHA	Ontario Hospital Association
OIG	Office of the Inspector General
OLAP	online analytical processing
OLTP	online transaction processing
ONC	Office of the National Coordinator for Health Information Technology
OP	outpatient
OPD	Outpatient Department
OPDIV	operating division
OPDRA	Office of Post-marketing Drug Risk Assessment
OPPS	Outpatient Prospective Payment System
OR	Operating Room

ORSOS	Operating Room Scheduling Office System
ORYX	JCAHO's quality program
OSHA	Occupational Safety and Health Administration
OT	occupational therapy
PACS	picture archiving and communication system
PACU	Post-Anesthesia Care Unit
PBC	prepared by client
PBM	pharmacy benefit manager
PBX	private branch exchange
PC	professional component (of work)
PCP	primary care physician
PCWRVU	professional component work relative value unit
PECOS	Provider Enrollment, Chain, and Ownership System
PGA	professional graphical adapter
PHO	physician-hospital organization
PHQ	patient health questionnaire
PICU	Psychiatric Intensive Care Unit
PL	procedural language
PM	performance management
PMPM	per member per month
POS	point-of-service organization
PPMC	physician practice management company
PPO	preferred provider organization
PPS	prospective payment system
PQI	prevention quality indicator
PRO	peer review organization
PSI	patient safety indicator
QFD	quality function deployment
QI	quality indicator
QIES	quality improvement evaluation system
QIO	quality improvement organization
QMS	quality management system
QuIC	Quality Interagency Coordinating Committee
QWL	quality of work life
RBRVS	resource-based relative value scale
RCM	revenue cycle management
RDRG	refined diagnostic-related group
RFID	radio frequency identification

RFP	request for proposal
RMAN	Recovery Manager
ROA	return on assets
ROE	return on equity
ROI	return on investment
RPQ	request for price quotation
RVU	relative value unit
SAMHSA	Substance Abuse and Mental Health Services Administration
SAN	storage area network
SAS	statistical analysis system
SCC	Standards Council of Canada
SECT	single-photon emission computerized tomography
SEER	Surveillance, Epidemiology, and End Results Program
SFAS	statement of financial accounting standards
SHPPS	School Health Policies and Programs Study
SIP	surgical infection prevention
SMI	service mix index
SMR	subsidiary medical record
SMSA	standard metropolitan statistical area
SNF	skilled nursing facility
SNI	system network interface
SNOMED	systematized nomenclature of medicine
SPC	statistical process control
SQL	Structured Query Language
SROM	spontaneous rupture of membranes
SRS	system requirements specification
STATE	State Tobacco Activities Tracking and Evaluation System
STDSS	sexually transmitted disease surveillance system
TASH	total available staff hours
TAT	test turnaround time
TC	technical component (of work)
TEP	technical expert panel
TPO	treatment, payment, or healthcare operations
TRIP	Translating Research Into Practice
TSM	Tivoli Storage Management
UAT	user acceptance testing
UCR	usual, customary, and reasonable
UMLS	Unified Medical Language System

UMR	unit medical record
UNAIDS	United Nations Program on HIV/AIDS
USC	usual source of care
USP	United States Pharmacopeia
USRDS	United States Renal Data System
VA	Department of Veterans Affairs
VHA	Veterans Health Administration
WACC	weighted average cost of capital
WHO	World Health Organization
WINS	Windows Internet Name Service
WVS	weighted value score
YRBSS	Youth Risk Behavior Surveillance System

Glossary

Access and service: A measure of how well a health plan provides its members with access to care with good customer service.

Access to care: Provision for timely and appropriate healthcare.

Accident: An event that involves damage to a defined system that disrupts the ongoing or future output of the system.

Accounts payable: Total of all monies owed by the organization.

Accounts receivable: Monies owed to the organization but not yet collected.

Accreditation: A decision awarded to a healthcare organization that is in compliance with established standards.

Accruals: Taxes or wages accumulated against current profits but not yet due to be paid.

Accuracy: The extent to which data are free of identifiable errors.

Active error: An error at the level of the frontline operator whose effects are felt almost immediately.

Activity-based costing: An accounting method used to estimate costs of a service or product by measuring the costs of the activities it takes to produce that service or product.

Acuity: The degree of psychosocial risk of health treatment or the degree of dependency or functional status of the patient.

Acute care hospital: A hospital that provides acute care services. Excludes discharges to long-term and rehabilitation hospitals.

Added value: The additional, tangible benefit derived by an organization through carrying out a business function or process.

Adjusted average per capita cost (AAPCC): The amount of funding a managed care plan receives from the Health Care Financing Administration to cover costs.

Administrative/billing data: Patient demographics; information about the episode of care such as admission source, length of stay, charges, discharge status; and diagnostic and procedural codes.

Administrative/financial measures: Performance measures that address the organizational structure for coordinating and integrating services, functions, or activities across operational components, including financial management.

Admission–discharge–transfer (ADT) system: A computer-based system used to track the gross movement of patients from their arrival to their departure within a medical enterprise. ADT systems are concerned primarily with patient demographics and provider information.

Adult day care program: A program providing supervision, medical and psychological care, and social activities for older adults who live at home or in another family setting but cannot be alone or prefer to be with others during the day.

Adverse event: An injury resulting from a medical intervention.

Agency for Healthcare Research and Quality (AHRQ): The health services research arm of the U.S. Department of Health and Human Services.

Affordable Care Act (ACA): Also known as Obamacare, the federal statute signed into law on March, 2010, that is part of the healthcare reform agenda of the Obama administration.

Aggregate: Measurement data collected and reported by organizations as a sum or total over a given time period or for certain groupings.

Algorithm: An ordered sequence of data element retrieval and aggregation through which numerator and denominator events or continuous variable values are identified by a measure.

Allied health personnel: Healthcare workers specially trained and licensed to assist and support the work of health professionals, such as dental assistants, dental technicians, medical record administrators, pharmacists' aides, and radiology technicians.

Allowable value: The predefined range of alphanumeric values that are valid for a data element in a database.

Allowance for doubtful accounts: An estimated amount of bad debt subtracted from a balance sheet's accounts receivable. This is a reserve for doubtful and bad accounts.

Ambulatory care: Healthcare services provided to patients on an ambulatory basis, rather than by admission to a hospital or other healthcare facility. Also called *outpatient care*.

Ambulatory payment classification (APC): A payment group under the Hospital Outpatient Prospective Payment System composed of procedures that are clinically similar and associated with similar resource requirements.

American Hospital Quest for Quality Prize: An American Hospital Association award that honors leadership and innovation in quality, safety, and commitment to patient care by hospitals and/or multihospital health systems.

American National Standards Institute (ANSI): A nonprofit organization that helps establish electronic data standards.

American Recovery and Reinvestment Act (ARRA): An economic stimulus package enacted in 2009 that included the HITECH Act.

Amortization: The gradual elimination of a liability in regular payments over a specified period of time. Alternatively, writing off an intangible asset investment over the projected life of the asset.

Ancillary services: Tests, procedures, and imaging and support services provided in a healthcare setting.

Assets: Money, merchandise, land, buildings, and equipment that the organization owns and that have monetary value.

Attestation: The part of the process to secure CMS EMR Incentive Program reimbursements that requires providers to prove (attest to) that they are meaningfully using a certified EMR.

Audit trail: A software tracking system used for data security. An audit trail is attached to a file each time it is opened so an operator can trace who has accessed a file and when.

Auditability: Performance measure data obtained from enrolled healthcare organizations are traceable at the individual case level so that performance measurement systems can adequately assess the quality of data.

Authentication: Proving, with some degree of certainty, a user's identity.

Average daily census: The average number of inpatients, excluding newborns, receiving care each day during a reporting period.

Average length of service (ALOS): Number of years in continuous, full-time employment or equivalent.

Backend process: A process that doesn't represent a healthcare institution's unique skills, knowledge, or processes. Typical backend processes include payroll, billing, and accounts payable.

Bad debt: Accounts receivable that will likely remain uncollectible and written off. Bad debts appear as an expense on the hospital's income statement, thus reducing net income.

Bad debt expense: Provision for actual or expected uncollectibles resulting from the extension of credit.

Bad outcome: Failure to achieve a desired outcome of care.

Balance sheet: A statement of the financial position of the enterprise at a particular time.

Balanced scorecard: An integrated framework for describing strategy through the use of linked performance measures in four balanced perspectives: financial, customer, internal process, and employee learning and growth.

Baseline: The starting point for defining needs.

Behavioral healthcare: Healthcare services organized to provide mental healthcare.

Benchmarking: The comparison of similar processes across organizations and industries to identify best practices, set improvement targets and measure progress.

Beneficiary: A person eligible for the coverage of healthcare services by either a public or private health insurance program.

Best of breed: The service provider that is best in its class of services.

Best practice: The most effective and desirable method of carrying out a function or process.

Binary: A system of expressing numerical values as 0s and 1s.

Binary outcome: Events or conditions that occur in one or two possible states—that is, 0 or 1. Such data are frequently encountered in medical research.

Bioinformatics: The use of computer-based methods, including large databases and related tools, to acquire, store, manage, and analyze biological data.

Biometrics: A method of verifying the identity of a user based on their fingerprints, facial features, retinal pattern, voice, or other personal characteristic.

Boxplot: A graph in which thin lines connect the highest and lowest data points to boxes that represent the two center quartiles on the graph.

Break-even analysis: A calculation of the approximate sales volume required to just cover costs, below which production would be unprofitable and above which it would be profitable.

Browser: A software program that interprets documents on the web.

Business intelligence (BI): Information technology practices and products concerned with gathering and analyzing financial and operational indicators.

Business process management (BPM): A business improvement strategy based on documenting, analyzing, and redesigning processes for greater performance.

Bylaws: Self-imposed rules that constitute a contract between a corporation and its members to conduct business in a particular way.

CAHPS: A comprehensive and evolving family of surveys, funded and managed by AHRQ, that ask consumers and patients to evaluate the interpersonal aspects of healthcare. CAHPS initially stood for the Consumer Assessment of Health Plans Study, but as the products have evolved beyond health plans, the acronym now stands alone as a registered brand name.

Capital budget: A summary of the anticipated purchases for the year.

Capital expenditure: An expenditure on tangible and intangible assets that will benefit more than one year of account.

Capitation: A payment structure where a caregiver is paid a set amount per patient in advance, regardless of how many procedures are performed.

Cardiac catheterization laboratory: Facilities offering special diagnostic procedures for cardiac patients.

Cascading: The process of developing aligned scorecards throughout an organization.

Case finding: The procedure for determining whether a case is potentially eligible for inclusion in the denominator of a measure.

Case management: A system of assessment, treatment planning, referral, and follow-up that ensures the provision of comprehensive and continuous services and the coordination of payment and reimbursement for care.

Case mix index (CMI): A severity statistic used as a weight for Medicare patients. CMI varies from 0.4 to over 16.0, with an average of 1.0.

Case mix: The collective pool of patients in a health system, including data on age, gender, and health status.

Cash flow: A measure of a hospital's financial health, equal to cash receipts minus cash payments over a given period of time. Alternatively, net profit plus amounts charged off for depreciation, depletion, and amortization.

Cash flow statement: A report on the impact of an organization's operating, investing, and financing activities on the cash flow over an accounting period.

Categorical variable: A categorical variable groups items into predefined discrete, noncontinuous classes.

Cause and effect: A linkage between items on a balanced scorecard. Cause and effect may be hypothetical.

Census day: A period of service between the census-taking hours on two successive calendar days, the day of discharge being counted only when the patient was admitted the same day.

Central tendency: A property of the distribution of a variable, usually measured by statistics such as the mean, median, and mode.

Change management: The set of structures, procedures, and rules governing the adoption and implementation of changes in the relationship between the customer and the service provider.

Children wellness program: A program that encourages the improved health status and healthful lifestyle of children through health education, exercise, nutrition, and health promotion.

Children's Online Privacy Protection Act (COPPA): The federal law that regulates the web-based collection and use of personal information gathered from or about children under age 13.

Chi-square: A test for statistical significance, typically applied to data in contingency tables.

Choice board: A web-based, multiuser ordering system in which a customer's order is sent to suppliers along the entire supply chain.

Claim: A bill for healthcare services.

Clearinghouse: A service that manages the claims and other electronic data from providers, verifies the information, and forwards the proper forms to the payers.

Client–server: A computer architecture in which the workload is split between desktop PCs or handheld wireless devices (clients) and more powerful or higher-capacity computers (servers) that are connected via a network such as the internet.

Clinic visit: A visits to a specialized medical unit that is responsible for the diagnosis and treatment of patients on an outpatient, non-emergency basis.

Clinical data–based severity adjustment methods: Techniques that quantify risks of short-term outcomes based on clinical data.

Clinical Laboratory Improvement Amendments (CLIA): A congressional amendment passed in 1988 that established quality standards for all laboratory testing.

Clinical laboratory personnel: Those healthcare professionals, technicians, and assistants staffing a healthcare facility where specimens are grown, tested, or evaluated and the results of such are recorded.

Clinical measures: Indicators designed to evaluate the processes or outcomes of care associated with the delivery of clinical services.

Clinical outcome: A change in signs or symptoms as a result of clinical intervention.

Clinical performance measure: A quality measure reflecting the degree to which a provider competently and safely delivers clinical services that are appropriate for the patient in the optimal time period.

Clinical performance: The degree of accomplishment of desired health objectives by a clinician or healthcare organization.

Clinical survey: A tool used to collect data from clinicians who provide care.

Closed formulary: A list of branded and generic prescription drugs that are approved for insurance coverage. Patients are required to pay more when they insist on brand-name drugs instead of less expensive generic drugs.

Closed Physician-Hospital Organization (PHO): A PHO that restricts physician membership to those practitioners who meet criteria for cost-effectiveness and/or high quality.

Cluster analysis: One of several computationally efficient techniques that can be used to identify patterns and relationships in large amounts of patient data.

Cognitive ergonomics: The applied science of equipment design, as for the workplace, intended to maximize productivity by reducing operator fatigue and discomfort.

Coinsurance: The portion of a covered claim that a patient must pay.

COLA: A nonprofit, physician-directed organization promoting quality and excellence in medicine and patient care through programs of voluntary education, achievement, and accreditation. COLA was established as a private alternative for physician office laboratories complying with the Clinical Laboratory Improvement Amendments of 1988.

Collusion: A fraudulent arrangement between two or more parties.

Commission: A type of finder's fee set by insurance brokers or agents for selling health plans.

Commission for Health Improvement (CHI): The National Health Service (NHS) inspectorate, responsible for reviewing clinical governance arrangements in NHS organizations.

Common carrier: Licensed utilities that provide communications services for a fee, under nondiscriminatory terms.

Common cause variation: Random variation inherent in every process.

Communications protocol: A set of standards designed to allow computers to exchange data.

Community healthcare: Diagnostic, therapeutic, and preventive healthcare services provided for individuals or families in the community for the purpose of promoting, maintaining, or restoring health or minimizing the effects of illness and disability.

Community Health Information Network (CHIN): Providers and payers within a specific area who are networked to exchange medical and administrative information among them, eliminating redundant data collection and reducing paperwork.

Community of practice: Groups whose members regularly engage in sharing and learning, based on common interests.

Comorbidities: Pre-existing diseases or conditions.

Comparison group: The group of healthcare organizations to which an individual healthcare organization is compared.

Comparison-level data: Aggregation of healthcare organization–level data to provide a standardized norm by which participating organizations can compare their performance.

Competitive insourcing: A process where internal employees may engage in bidding to compete with competitive, third-party bidders for a defined scope of work.

Competitive reward model: A program that rewards relative performance.

Complications: Conditions arising after the beginning of healthcare observation and treatment that modifies the course of the patient's health or illness and the intervention/care required.

Composite measure: A measure that combines the results of all process measures with a set into a single rating.

Computerized physician order entry (CPOE): An electronic prescribing system that enables a physician to order through a computer rather than on paper.

Confidence interval: A range of values containing the true value of the parameter being estimated with a certain degree of confidence.

Configuration: The operational characteristics of a performance measurement system.

Confounding factors: Intervening variables that distort the true relationship between/among the variables of interest.

Consumer informatics: Computer-based information available to the general public.

Continuity: The degree to which the care for the patient is coordinated among practitioners, among organizations, and over time.

Continuous variable: A measure in which each individual value for the measure can fall anywhere along a continuous scale.

Contract: A binding agreement made between two or more parties that is enforceable at law.

Contract managed: General day-to-day management of an entire organization by another organization under a formal contract.

Contractor: A firm or person who has entered into a contract to supply goods and/or services.

Control chart: A form of line chart that includes control limits based on plus or minus three standard deviations or sigmas from the centerline. There are heuristics for determining when an observed variation is statistically significant.

Controlled vocabulary: A terminology system unambiguously mapped to concepts.

Convergence: The merging of all data and all media into a single digital form.

Coordination of benefits (COB): A verification system used to make sure a claim is not paid twice.

Co-payment: The flat fee that a patient pays, usually at the time of service.

Core competency: The healthcare organization's unique skills, knowledge, and processes.

Core measure set: A grouping of performance measures carefully selected to provide, when viewed together, a robust picture of the care provided in a given area.

Cost shifting: A leveling method where one patient group is charged more to make up for another group's underpayment or inability to pay.

Cost–benefit analysis: A technique designed to determine the feasibility of a project or plan by quantifying its costs and benefits.

Cost-to-charge ratio: The ratio of hospital cost to what is charged to patients and third-party payers for services. Medicare has explicit guidelines for establishing cost-to-charge ratios.

Credentialing: The examination of a healthcare professional's credentials, practice history and medical certification or license.

Criteria: Expected levels of achievement or specifications against which performance or quality may be compared.

Critical access hospital: Hospitals with a patient census of less than 25 and that are located more than 35 miles from a hospital or another critical access hospital, or are certified by the state as being a necessary provider of healthcare services to residents in the area.

Critical path: The shortest path to the final product or service in resource scheduling. The critical path represents the minimum length of time in which a project can be completed.

Cube: A multidimensional data source that contains measures (data) organized by dimension.

Current assets: Cash, short-term investment, accounts receivable, inventory, prepaid expenses, and other assets that can be converted into cash within a year.

Current liabilities: Liability that must be paid within a year, including accounts payable, wages and salaries, taxes, and mortgage payments.

Current procedural terminology (CPT): A uniform coding system for healthcare procedures developed by the American Medical Association (AMA) and used when submitting claims for healthcare to third-party payers. CPT coding assigns a five-digit code to each service or procedure provided by a physician.

Current status of development: The amount of work completed to date relative to the final implementation of a particular measure.

Current use of the measure: A measure is considered to be in current use if at least one healthcare organization has used the measure to evaluate or report on the quality of care within the last three years.

Customer perspective: One of the four standard perspectives used with the balanced scorecard.

Customer relationship management (CRM): The dynamic process of managing a patient–healthcare organization relationship. Patients are encouraged to continue mutually beneficial commercial exchanges and are dissuaded from participating in exchanges that are unprofitable to the organization.

Customer segment: A homogeneous group of similar patients with similar needs, wants, lifestyles, interaction opportunities, profiles, and purchase cycles.

Cycle time: The time it takes to convert an idea into a new product or service or to improve an existing product or service.

Dashboard: A graphical user interface to key performance indicator data.

Data collection: The act or process of capturing raw or primary data from a single or number of sources.

Data analytics: The process of inspecting, cleaning, transforming, and modeling data with the goal of discovering useful information and ultimately of supporting decision making.

Data editing: The process of correcting erroneous or incomplete existing data, exclusive of data entry input edits.

Data element: A discrete piece of data, such as patient birth date or principal diagnosis.

Data entry: The process by which data are transcribed or transferred into an electronic format.

Data maintenance: The efforts required to keep database files and supporting documentation accurate.

Data mart: An organized, searchable database system, organized according to the user's likely needs.

Data mining: The process of studying the contents of large databases in order to discover new data relationships that may produce new insights on outcomes, alternate treatments, or effects of treatment.

Data point: The representation of a value for a set of observations or measurements at a specific time interval.

Data quality: The accuracy and completeness of measured data on performance in the context of the analytical purposes for which they will be used.

Data repository: A database acting as an information storage facility. A repository does not have the analysis or querying functionality of a warehouse.

Data sources: The primary source documents used for data collection.

Data transmission: The process by which data are electronically sent from one organization to another.

Data warehouse: A central database, frequently very large, that can provide authorized users with access to a cleaned, organized subset of the organizations data. A data warehouse is usually provided with data from a variety of noncompatible sources.

Database: An organized, comprehensive collection of variables and their values.

Database management system (DBMS): A system to store, process, and manage data in a systematic way.

Day of care: A period of service between the census-taking hours on two successive calendar days, the day of discharge being counted only when the patient was admitted the same day.

Days hold: Number of accounts still within the specified number of days after discharge prior to billing.

Debt service: The series of payments of interest and principal required on a debt over a given period of time.

Decision-effective date: The date of the accreditation decision awarded to an organization following an accreditation survey.

Decision support system (DSS): An application for analyzing large quantities of data and performing a wide variety of calculations and projections.

Decision tree analysis: A graphical process used to select the best course of action in cases of uncertainty.

Defined allowable value: The predefined range of alphanumeric values that are valid for a data element in a database.

Defined measure: A structured measure with defined populations that measure specific events or values.

Demand management: A program administered by managed care organizations or provider organizations to monitor and process initial member requests for clinical information and services.

Denominator data elements: Those data elements required to construct the denominator.

Denominator event: The event or state that defines a case as eligible for inclusion in the denominator.

Denominator excluded populations: Detailed information describing the populations that should not be included in the denominator.

Denominator included populations: Detailed information describing the population(s) that the denominator intends to measure.

Denominator sampling frame: The list of all cases potentially eligible for inclusion in the denominator, from which a more highly specified selection of cases will be made.

Denominator statement: A statement that depicts the population evaluated by the performance measure.

Denominator time window: The time period in which cases are reviewed for inclusion in the denominator.

Denominator verification: The extent to which the entire population of interest, and only the population of interest, is identified through data collection.

Depreciation: The decline in the value of a fixed asset over its useful life.

Diagnosis hold: Number of accounts not yet coded in medical records.

Diagnosis-related group (DRG): A system of reimbursement by the Health Care Financing Administration based on a patient's primary diagnosis, length of stay, secondary diagnosis, surgical procedure, age, and types of services required. This case-mix classification system is used primarily in the United States as a method of funding hospitals.

Digital signature: An encrypted digital tag added to an electronic communication to verify the identity of a customer. Also known as an electronic signature.

Direct cost: That portion of cost that is directly expended in providing a service.

Disabled: Persons with physical or mental disabilities that affect or limit their activities of daily living and may require special accommodations.

Discharge instructions: A quality measure that reflects the percentage of patients with heart failure who are given information about their condition and care when they leave the hospital.

Discount rate: The rate at which member banks may borrow short-term funds directly from a Federal Reserve Bank.

Discriminatory capability: The extent to which an indicator demonstrates variation across multiple healthcare organizations.

Disenrollment: The act of terminating the membership of a person or group in a health plan.

Disruptive technology: A technology that causes a major shift in the normal way of doing things and that improves with time. PCs, digital cameras, and cell phones are disruptive technologies.

DMADV: A Six Sigma strategy divided into five phases: define, measure, analyze, design, and verify.

DMAIC: A Six Sigma quality improvement strategy described by five phases: define, measure, analyze, improve, and control.

Downsizing: Reduction in employee headcount.

Drug price review (DPR): A monthly report that lists the average whole-sale prices of prescription drugs.

Due diligence: A thorough effort to intercept potential problems before they occur.

Ease of use: Regarding a user interface, the ease or efficiency with which the interface can be used.

Economic Darwinism: Survival of the fittest—the most economically successful companies in the marketplace.

Economic value added (EVA): The after-tax cash flow generated by a business minus the cost of the capital it has deployed to generate that cash flow.

Economies of scale: Reduction in the costs of production due to increasing production capacity.

Efficacy: The degree to which the care of the patient has been shown to accomplish the desired or projected outcome(s).

Electronic data interchange (EDI): An instance of data being sent electronically between parties, normally according to predefined industry standards.

Electronic health record (EHR): An electronic record of a patient's medical history, medications, and other pertinent health data. Need not be hospital-centric, as is the case with an EMR.

Electronic medical record (EMR): A hospital-centric, electronic record of a patient's hospital chart. This typically includes medical, social, and family histories, medications, lab results, and other data collected at the hospital.

Electronic submission: The process whereby performance measure data are transferred electronically between information systems.

Eligibility: The ability to be part of a healthcare plan, with specific benefits for which a member qualifies and the time frame of coverage.

Emergency Care Research Institute (ECRI): An independent nonprofit health services research agency.

Emergency medical services: Clinical services specifically designed, staffed, and equipped for the emergency care of patients.

Emergency medical technicians/paramedics: Personnel trained and certified to provide basic emergency care and life support under the supervision of physicians and/or nurses.

Emergency room visit: A visit to the emergency unit.

Employee benefits: Social Security, group insurance, retirement benefits, workman's compensation, and unemployment insurance.

Employee contribution: The portion of health plan premiums paid by an employee to the company's contracted payer.

Employer mandate: For companies that provide health insurance for their employees, this stipulation forces the company to pay for at least part of the insurance premium for each employee.

Encryption: The process of encoding data to prevent someone without the proper key from understanding the data, even though they may have access to the data.

Enforceability: The conditions under which the terms, conditions, and obligations of the parties under an agreement will be adopted and confirmed by a court of competent jurisdiction.

Enrollment: In the context of the Affordable Care Act, enrollment is the act of selecting a particular coverage plan with a healthcare insurance provider.

Enrolled organization: An organization contractually committed to participation in a performance measurement system.

Enrollee: A member of a health plan or a member's qualifying dependent.

Enrollment assistance services: A program that provides enrollment assistance for patients who are potentially eligible for public health insurance programs such as Medicaid, State Children's Health Insurance, or local/state indigent care programs.

Enterprise resource planning (ERP): The activities supported by software that help an enterprise manage product planning, parts purchasing, maintaining inventories, interacting with suppliers, providing customer service, and tracking orders.

Episode of care (EOC): Healthcare services provided for a specific illness during a set time period.

Equipment management: The selection, delivery, setup, and maintenance of equipment to meet patients' needs, as well as the education of patients in its use.

Ernest A. Codman Award: An award given to organizations and individuals in the use of process and outcomes measures to improve their performance and quality of care.

Error: Failure of a planned action to be completed as intended or the use of a wrong plan to achieve an aim; the accumulation of errors results in accidents.

Established patient: A patient who has received professional services within the past three years.

Excluded populations: Detailed information describing the populations that should not be included in the indicator.

Executive information system: A system that allows executives to analyze company data and reach management conclusions through decision-making tools, much as a physician might use a decision support system to narrow diagnosis options.

Expense: The cost of doing business.

Experience rating: A method of determining a company's health insurance premiums by estimating the future healthcare risks of its employees.

Explanation of benefits (EOB): A document that defines the portions of the service that are paid by insurance and the amount the patient has to pay.

External comparison at a point in time: A comparison using the same measure for multiple comparable entities.

External comparison of time trends: A comparison using the same measure for multiple comparable entities tracking change over time.

External data source: A repository for data that exists outside of the measurement system's control.

External standards: Performance measurement systems developed by government entities, accrediting bodies, or any regulatory entities so that performance data are comparable across measurement systems.

Extraction, transformation, and loading (ETL): The data acquisition process from source systems into a data warehouse.

Extranet: A private network using the internet protocol to share business information or operations with vendors, customers, and/or other businesses.

Food and Drug Administration Safety and Innovation Act (FDASIA): Section 618 of the act-directed development of risk-based regulatory frameworks for health IT.

Fee schedule: A list of maximum fees, per service, a provider will be reimbursed within a fee-for-service payment system.

Fee-for-service: A traditional method of paying for medical services. A physician charges a fee for each service provided, and the insurer or patient pay all or part of that fee.

Financial perspective: One of the four standard perspectives used with a balanced scorecard, often viewed as constraints within which the organization must operate.

Financial statement: A written report that quantitatively describes the financial health of a company. This includes an income statement and a balance sheet, and often also includes a cash flow statement.

Firewall: A software and/or hardware security system that allows or denies access to information and the transfer of information from one network to another based on predefined access rules.

Fisher's exact test: A statistical test used on contingency tables, more accurate than the chi-square test.

Fixed assets: Land and physical properties used in the creation of economic activity by the enterprise.

Fixed cost: A cost that does not vary depending on production or sales levels, such as rent, property tax, insurance, or interest expense.

Focus: The activity or area on which a performance measure centers attention.

Forecasting: A mathematical method of extrapolating historical performance data to aid in planning. As with weather forecasting, the further into the future the forecast, the less certain the results.

Format: The specification of the character length of a specific data element.

Formulary: A list of pharmaceutical products and dosages deemed by a healthcare organization to be the best, most economical treatments.

Franklin Award of Distinction: Award for a case management system that demonstrates excellence in building collaboration among the various professional and technical staff in the hospital to focus on case management and performance measurement results having a positive effect on patient care.

Frequency distribution: The division of a sample of observations into a number of classes, together with the number of observations in each class.

Functional specification: A document that incorporates and crystallizes the requirements specifications and specifies exactly what a software and/or hardware system will deliver.

Functional status: A measure of an individual's ability to perform normal activities of life.

Full-time equivalent (FTE): A measure of employee time devoted to work, typically eight hours per day.

Gantt chart: A graphical production scheduling method that shows the lengths of various production stages.

Gap analysis: The process of determining the variance between business requirements and system capabilities.

General data elements: The group of data elements used to link healthcare organization level to comparison group data.

Generally accepted accounting principles (GAAP): The conventions, rules, and procedures that define accepted accounting practice, as defined by the Financial Accounting Standards Board.

Geographically defined: Persons located within a specified boundary.

Government Performance and Results Act (GPRA): Legislation that requires federally funded agencies to develop and implement an accountability system based on performance measurement.

Gross profit: A financial indicator equal to profit before expenses, interest, and taxes have been deducted.

Gross revenue: Total revenue less cost of goods sold.

Gross sales: Total invoice value of sales, before deducting for customer discounts, allowances, or returns.

Group model HMO: A form of HMO where a partnership or company provides services and pays for the facility and salaries.

Group Purchasing Organization: An organization whose primary function is to negotiate contracts for the purpose of purchasing for members of the group or has a central supply site for its members.

Half-life: The time in which half of the devices or applications in a given population fail or become useless due to obsolescence.

Microsystems: The multiple small units of caregivers, administrators, and other staff who deliver care and services.

HCPCS: The HCFA Common Procedural Coding System.

Health Care Financing Administration (HCFA): The branch of the U.S. Department of Health and Human Services that administers Medicare and the federal portion of Medicaid.

Healthcare network: An entity that provides, or provides for, integrated health services to a defined population or individuals.

Health care organization (HCO): Entity that provides, coordinates, and/or insures health and medical services for people.

Healthcare system: A corporate body that owns, leases, religiously sponsors, and/or manages health provider facilities.

Health episode statistics (HES): A database containing details of all patients admitted to NHS hospitals in England.

Health maintenance organization (HMO): An affiliation of independent practitioners that contracts with patients to provide comprehensive healthcare for a fixed periodic payment specified in advance.

Health plan: A person's specific health benefits package or the organization that provides such a package.

Health Plan Employer Data and Information Set (HEDIS): NCQA's tool used by health plans to collect data about the quality of care and service they provide.

Health risk state: Behavior associated with negative medical consequences.

Health status measures: Indicators that assess the functional well-being of specific populations, both in general and in relation to specific conditions.

Healthcare informatics: The use of computer-based tools, applications, and communications to interact with and manage health-related data.

Healthcare Insurance Portability and Accountability Act (HIPAA): The U.S. government regulation that holds healthcare facilities responsible for bringing legacy IT systems into stringent compliance and ensuring the security of patient records.

Heuristic: A rule of thumb.

Health Information Technology for Economic and Clinical Health (HITECH) Act: Part of the American Recovery and Reinvestment Act of 2009 that promotes the adoption and meaningful use of health information technology.

HL7: A standard interface for exchanging and translating data between computer systems.

Home Healthcare Agency: An organization that arranges for and provides necessary healthcare services in a patient's home.

Horizontal analysis: The percentage change in indicator value from a previous year—that is, [(subsequent − previous)/previous] × 100.

Hospital alliance: Hospital groups that agree to buy equipment and services jointly rather than incurring the costs separately.

Hospital information system (HIS): A computer-based system that usually includes patient tracking, billing, and administrative programs and also may include clinical features.

Human capital: Employee knowledge, skills, and relationships.

Human factors: The study of the interrelationships between humans, the tools they use, and the environment in which they live and work.

In process: Indicates NCQA has reviewed the health plan for the first time and is in the process of making a decision on the accreditation outcome.

Incentive and reward program: A program that rewards and encourages providers to improve quality and efficiency.

Incidence: A rate showing how many new cases of a disease occurred in a population during a specified interval of time, usually expressed as the number of new cases per unit time per fixed number of people.

Incident to services: Those services furnished as an integral, although incidental, part of the physician's personal professional services in the course of diagnosis or treatment of an injury or illness.

Included populations: Detailed information describing the population(s) that the indicator intends to measure.

Income statement: An accounting of sales, expenses, and net profit for a given period.

Incurred but not reported (IBNR): When services have been delivered but the insurer has not processed the claim.

Indemnification: A method of shifting legal liability from one party to another by contract.

Indemnity insurer: An insurance company that pays for the medical care of its insured but does not deliver healthcare.

Independent practice association (IPA): A type of HMO that contracts with a group of associated physicians for services to its members.

Index: A type of composite measure that adds up individual scores on several items for an individual and divides this sum by the number items scored.

Indirect cost: A cost that is indirectly expended in providing a service.

Individually identifiable health information (IIHI): Health information that can be associated with an individual.

Infrastructure: The system of servers, cables, and other hardware, together with the software that ties it together, for the purpose of supporting the operation of devices on a network.

Initiatives: The specific programs, activities, projects, or actions an organization will undertake in an effort to meet performance targets.

Inpatient care: Services delivered to a patient who needs physician care for at least 24 hours, usually in a hospital.

Insourcing: The transfer of an outsourced function to an internal department of the customer, to be managed entirely by employees.

Institute of medicine (IOM): A private, nonprofit institution that provides information and advice concerning health and science policy under a congressional charter.

Institutionalization: The care delivered in a hospital, rehabilitation hospital, or nursing home, from admission to discharge.

Institutionalized adults: Persons in long-term care or nursing homes.

Insurance hold: Number of accounts waiting for insurance verification.

Intangible asset: Something of value that cannot be physically touched, such as a brand, franchise, trademark, or patent.

Integrated delivery system (IDS): A unified healthcare system that provides physician, hospital, and ambulatory care services for its members by contracting with several provider sites and health plans.

Integration: The process of bringing together related data from different sources to arrange it by customer.

Intellectual property: Know-how, trade secrets, copyrights, patents, trademarks, and service marks.

Interface: The procedures, codes, and protocols that enable two systems to interact for a meaningful exchange of information.

Intermediate care facility: A place that provides medical care to patients who don't need to be in a hospital.

Internal process perspective: One of the four standard perspectives used with a balanced scorecard, used to monitor the effectiveness of key processes the organization must excel at in order to continue adding value for patients and shareholders.

Internal standards: Performance measurement quality standards tailored to a specific healthcare organization.

Internal time comparison: A comparison using the same measure in the same organization at two or more points in time to evaluate present or prior performance.

International Classification of Diseases, 9th revision, with clinical modifications (ICD-9-CM): A coding system developed in the United States, based on the ICD-9 code developed by the World Health Organization. ICD-9-CM codes provide a standard for comparison of birth, death, and disease data.

International Classification of Diseases, 10th Revision (ICD-10): A list that assigns codes to types of illnesses or conditions. Whereas CPT codes represent procedures and other services, ICD-10 codes represent diagnoses.

International Organization for Standardization (ISO): An international organization that establishes standards in a variety of areas, including quality management (see ISO 9000).

Inventory: The stock of goods on hand that is for sale.

ISO 9000: The family of ISO standards concerned with quality management.

John M. Eisenberg Award for Patient Safety and Quality: An award that recognizes the major achievements of individuals and organizations in improving patient safety and quality.

Joint Commission on Accreditation of Healthcare Organizations (JCAHO): A commission that defines standards concerning the content and quality of medical records, as well as requirements for organization-wide information management processes that must be followed to qualify for participation in the Medicare and Medicaid programs.

Joint venture: A contractual arrangement between two or more parties forming an unincorporated business.

Just-in-time (JIT): A manufacturing philosophy in which raw materials arrive no earlier than they are required to reduce costs and inefficiencies associated with a large inventory.

Kaizen: A Japanese quality improvement philosophy named after the phrase "continuous improvement."

Karnofsky performance score (KPS): A score used to quantify a patient's general well-being, often used to determine whether a cancer patient can receive chemotherapy. The score ranges from 0% (death) to 100% (normal, no complaints, no signs of disease).

Key performance indicators (KPIs): Core measures that gauge the performance of an organization in a particular area, in terms of how the organization has performed in the past and how it is currently performing.

Knowledge engineering: The process of extracting knowledge from an expert with enough detail and completeness that the knowledge can be imparted to others or to an information system.

Knowledge management: A deliberate, systematic business optimization strategy that selects, distills, stores, organizes, packages, and communicates information essential to the business of a company in a manner that improves employee performance and corporate competitiveness.

Knowledge organization: An organization that creates, acquires, transfers, and retains information.

Knowledge repository: A central locations of information on best practices

Knowledge workers: Employees hired primarily for what they know.

Knowledgebase: A database that contains information about other data contained in the database.

Laboratory: Hospital-based main laboratories or point-of-care testing, free-standing laboratories, embryology laboratories, reference laboratories, blood banks, and donor centers.

Lagging indicator: A performance measure that represents the consequences of actions previously taken.

Latency: The delay inherent in a system.

Latent error: An error in the design, organization, training, or maintenance that leads to operator errors and whose effects typically lie dormant in the system for lengthy periods of time.

Leading indicators: Measures considered drivers of future performance. A predictive measure.

Lean manufacturing: A quality methodology focused on eliminating all waste from the manufacturing process.

Legacy system: An existing information system in which an enterprise has invested considerable time and money.

Leverage: The degree to which an organization assumes a larger proportion of debt than the amount invested by its owners.

Liabilities: Everything a company owes a creditor. The sum of current liabilities and short-term debt.

Liquidity: Capacity to pay debts as they come due.

Local area network (LAN): A network of computer and peripherals in close proximity, usually in the same building.

Localization: The process of adapting a website to a particular country or region.

Logical Observation Identifiers Names and Codes (LOINC): Universal identifiers for laboratory and other clinical observations.

Logistic regression: A form of regression analysis used when the response variable is a binary variable.

Long-term care pharmacy: Services that include the procurement, preparation, dispensing, and distribution of pharmaceutical products, and ongoing monitoring and assistance in managing the resident's clinical status and outcomes related drug therapy.

Long-term care: The health and personal care services provided to chronically ill, aged, physically disabled, or learning-disabled persons in an institution or in the place of residence.

Long-term debt: Financial obligations that come due more than one year from the date of the balance sheet statement.

Lost opportunity cost: The cost of not applying resources to toward an alternative investment.

Loyalty: A positive inner feeling or emotional bond between a patient and healthcare organization or provider.

Magnet hospital: An award presented by the American Nurses Credentialing Center (ANCC) to organized nursing services.

Malcolm Baldrige National Quality Award: An award established by Congress to promote quality awareness, to recognize the quality and business achievements of U.S. organizations, and to publicize the award winners' successful performance strategies.

Managed behavioral health (MBHO): A delivery system for behavioral health concerns that includes managed care services.

Managed Behavioral Healthcare Organization (MBHO): A system of behavioral healthcare delivery that manages the quality, utilization, and cost of services, and which measures performance in the area of mental and substance abuse disorders.

Managed care: A healthcare system and ideology based on prepaid membership instead of fee-for-service payment each time a service is delivered.

Managed care organization (MCO): A general term for health plans that provide healthcare in return for preset monthly payments and coordinate care through a defined network of primary care physicians and hospitals.

Managed care plans: Health insurance plans intended to reduce healthcare costs through a variety of mechanisms.

Managed care: The assumption of responsibility and accountability for the health of a defined population and the simultaneous acceptance of financial risk.

Management services organization (MSO): A corporation, owned by the hospital or a physician-hospital joint venture, that provides management services to one or more medical group practices.

Margin of safety: An excess of intrinsic value over market price.

Marginal cost: The change in cost as the result of one more or less unit of output.

Marketing: The process associated with promoting products or services for sale, traditionally involving product, price, place, and promotion.

Mass customization: Providing products as per customer specifications using traditional manufacturing techniques.

Master patient index: A database that collects a patient's various hospital identification numbers, perhaps from the blood lab, radiology, admission and so on, and keeps them under a single, enterprise-wide identification number.

Material requirements planning (MRP): A strategy to increase manufacturing efficiency by managing the production schedule, reducing inventory, increasing cash flow, and delivering products in a timely manner.

Mean: The average value of a sample.

Meaningful Use: A Medicare and Medicaid program that awards incentives for using certified EHRs to improve patient care.

Measure: A standard used to evaluate and communicate performance against expected results.

Measure information form: A tool used to provide specific clinical and technical information on a measure.

Measure-related feedback: Measure-related information on performance that is available, on a timely basis, to organizations actively participating in the performance measurement system for use in the organization's ongoing efforts to improve patient care and organization performance.

Median: The middle value when the numbers are arranged in order of magnitude.

Medicaid: A joint federal and state healthcare program for low-income or disabled persons.

Medical informatics: The use of computer-based tools to assist with core clinical functions, decision support, and research functions.

Medical record: Data obtained from the records or documentation maintained on a patient in any healthcare setting.

Medical record hold: Number of accounts not yet abstracted in medical records.

Medical savings account: A private equity fund, much like an individual retirement account, set up to help cover future healthcare expenses, forming medical financial security regardless of workplace health plans.

Medically uninsured: Individuals or groups with no or inadequate health insurance coverage.

Medicare: The federal government's healthcare program for all persons over the age of 65 and for younger persons who have disabilities and cannot work.

Metadata: Data about data. How the structures and calculation rules are stored, information on data sources, definitions, quality, transformations, date of last update, and user access privileges.

Minority groups: A subgroup having special characteristics within a larger group, often bound together by special ties that distinguish it from the larger group.

Mirroring: Two identical files or databases created and updated simultaneously so an exact duplicate exists at all times.

Missing data: When there are no values present for one or more data elements that are required for calculating and/or risk adjusting a core measure.

Mission critical: Data relating to essential business operations.

Mission statement: Defines the core purpose of the organization.

Mode: The most frequently occurring value for a data element.

Model-based approach to risk adjustment: A statistical technique that uses a mathematical model to describe the relationship between an outcome and a set of explanatory variables that are used to study and characterize the data.

Morbidity: A measurement of illness or accident risk, based on categories of age, region, occupation, and others.

Mortality: Statistical death rates, usually broken down by age or gender.

Mortgage: A legal document that pledges property to cover debt.

Multivariate analysis: The analysis of the simultaneous relationships among variables.

National Committee for Quality Assurance (NCQA): A nonprofit organization that acts as a watchdog for the quality of care delivered by managed care plans and physician organizations. Its accreditation process includes HEDIS and patient satisfaction surveys.

National Institute of Standards and Technology (NIST): A federal agency within the Commerce Department's Technology Administration whose primary mission is to develop and promote measurements, standards, and technology to enhance productivity, facilitate trade, and improve quality of life.

National Library of Medicine (NLM): The largest medical library and a branch of the National Institutes of Health (NIH).

National Patient Safety Goals: A series of specified actions that accredited organizations are expected to take in order to prevent medical errors.

National Quality Forum (NQF): The independent, voluntary, consensus-based member organization that endorses standardized quality measures.

National Quality Improvement Goals: Standardized performance measures that can be applied across accredited healthcare organizations.

National Quality Measures Clearinghouse (NQMC): A public repository for evidence-based quality measures and measure sets sponsored by the Agency for Healthcare Research and Quality, U.S. Department of Health and Human Services.

Net earnings: The amount left over after deducting all due bills for the accounting period and paying off all due interest and federal taxes.

Net income: Revenues less expenses.

Net patient revenue: Net revenue from patients, third-party payers, and others for services rendered.

Net present value (NPV): The total present value of all cash flows, discounted to present day dollars. Enables managers to evaluate investments in today's dollars.

Net profit: Revenues minus taxes, interest, depreciation, and other expenses.

Net revenue: Gross revenue adjusted for deductions and expenses.

Net worth: Total assets minus total liabilities of an individual or company. Also called *owner's equity*, *shareholders' equity*, or *net assets*.

Network: A group of hospitals, physicians, other providers, insurers and/or community agencies that voluntarily work together to coordinate and deliver health services.

Network Model HMO: A health maintenance organization that contracts with multiple groups of physicians for care delivery.

New patient: One who has not received professional services from the physician, or another physician of the same specialty who belongs to the same group practice, within the past three years.

Noncompetitive reward model: A program that rewards absolute performance based on fixed targets or benchmarks.

Nonoperating revenue: Investment income, extraordinary gains, and other nonoperating gains.

Nonweighted score: A combination of the values of several items into a single summary value for each case.

Normalization: The process of reducing a complex data structure into its simplest, most stable structure. Normalization is often a prerequisite for an efficient relational database design.

Notes payable: Money borrowed by the organization that is to be repaid within 1 year.

Numerator: The upper portion of a fraction used to calculate a rate, proportion, or ratio.

Numerator data elements: Those data elements necessary or required to construct the numerator.

Numerator excluded populations: Detailed information describing the populations that should not be included in the numerator.

Numerator statement: A statement that depicts the portion of the denominator population that satisfies the conditions of the performance measure to be an indicator event.

Numerator time window: The time period in which cases are reviewed for inclusion in the numerator.

Objective: A concise statement describing the specific things an organization must do well in order to execute its strategy.

Observation service: A service furnished on a hospital's premises that is reasonable and necessary to evaluate an outpatient's condition or determine the need for a possible admission to the hospital as an inpatient.

Occupied bed day: A period of service between the census-taking hours on two successive calendar days, the day of discharge being counted only when the patient was admitted the same day.

Office-based surgery: Small organizations or practices composed of four or fewer physicians performing surgical procedures.

Ongoing data quality review process: A data quality review process in operation and that is intended to continue for as long as data are accepted into the database.

Open architecture: A network design that allows integration of various different types of computers and databases.

Operational data store: Where operational information from different systems is integrated in near real time.

Outcome measure: A measure that indicates the result of the performance of a function or process.

Outcome of care: The health state of a patient resulting from healthcare.

Outcomes: An assessment of a treatment's effectiveness by considering its success as a care solution as well as its cost, side effects, and risk.

Outcomes management: A program used to determine the clinical end results according to defined various categories and then promote the use of those categories that yield improved outcomes.

Outlier: A case in which costs far exceed those of a typical case within a diagnostic-related group (DRG).

Outlier payments: Supplements to prospective payments to defray some of the expenses in caring for the most costly cases.

Outpatient prospective payment system (OPPS): A prospective payment system established by the Balanced Budget Act of 1997 in which all services paid are classified into groups called *ambulatory payment classifications* or APCs. A payment rate is established for each APC. Services in each APC are similar clinically and in terms of the resources they require.

Outpatient surgery: Scheduled surgical services provided to patients who do not remain in the hospital overnight.

Outpatient visit: A visit by a patient who is not lodged in the hospital while receiving medical, dental, or other services.

Outsourcing: Entrusting a business process to an external services provider for a significant period of time.

Out-tasking: A limited form of outsourcing in which a task is contracted out to a consultant or other service provider.

Overhead: The expense of running the business as opposed to the direct costs of personnel and materials used to produce the end result.

Parameter: Any characteristic of a population that can be inferred.

Parent Organization: The primary site of care for a healthcare organization. An organization may have multiple locations of care accredited under one parent organization.

Pathology and clinical laboratory services: A service of a healthcare organization that is equipped to examine material derived from the human body to provide information for use in the diagnosis, prevention, or treatment of disease.

Patient accounting system: Software that records charges to patients, creates billing forms, and maintains payment records.

Patient demographics: Patient age, ethnicity, gender, and geographic location.

Patient experience of care: A patient experience is a report by a patient concerning observations of and participation in healthcare.

Patient factor: A variable describing some characteristic of individual patients that may influence healthcare-related outcomes.

Patient-level data: Collection of data elements that depict the healthcare services provided to a patient.

Patient survey: Data obtained from patients and/or their family members/significant others.

Payer: A company or an agency that purchases health services.

Payroll expenses: Payroll for all personnel including medical and dental residents, interns, and trainees.

Peak debt service: The largest annual interest expense and principal payments on existing debt.

Perception of care: Satisfaction measures that focus on the delivery of clinical care from the patient's/family's/caregiver's perspective.

Performance management: The skillful accomplishment of business through the effective use of resources.

Performance measure: A quantitative tool that provides an indication of an organization's performance in relation to a specified process or outcome.

Performance measurement system: A system of automated databases that facilitates performance improvement in healthcare organizations through the collection and dissemination of process and/or outcome measures of performance.

Performance measurements: The collected results of a healthcare organization's actual performance over a specified time.

Perspective: In balanced scorecard vernacular, a category of performance measures. The standard four perspectives are *financial, customer, internal process,* and *employee learning and growth.*

PERT chart: A method for project planning by analyzing the time required for each step.

Pervasive computing: The anytime, anyplace access of computational power and data, in an unobtrusive form.

Pharmaceutical services: Those services provided directly or through contract with another organization that procure, prepare, preserve, compound, dispense, or distribute pharmaceutical products, and monitor the patient's clinical status.

Pharmacists: Those persons legally qualified by education and training to engage in the practice of pharmacy.

Physician group practices/clinics: Any groups of three or more full-time physicians organized in a legally recognized entity for the provision of healthcare services, sharing space, equipment, personnel, and records for both patient care and business management, and who have a predetermined arrangement for the distribution of income.

Physician-hospital organization (PHO): A system where a hospital and its physician groups jointly own the organization. The PHO as an entity then assumes the responsibility of arranging contracts with managed care plans and care facilities.

Physician practice organization (PPO): A system where insurance companies, employers, and other healthcare buyers arrange lower fees with select physicians and facilities.

Picture archiving and communications system (PACS): A system that uses an image server to exchange X-rays, CT scans, and other medical images over a network.

Point of service (POS): An indemnity-type option offered by HMOs in which members can refer themselves outside the plan and still get some coverage.

Point of sale (POS): The device that is the first point in a financial transaction.

Point-of-service collections as a fraction of goal: Percentage of target monies collected at the time of service.

Population: A complete set of actual or potential observations.

Portal: A website that offers a broad array of resources and services, from email to online shopping. Most of the popular search engines have transformed themselves into web portals to attract a larger audience.

Positron emission tomography (PET): A nuclear medicine imaging technology used to produce composite pictures based on metabolic activity or blood flow.

Poverty populations: Persons living below the standard level of living of the community.

Practice sanctions: Penalties, ranging from practice limitations to the non-renewal of contracts, for the failure of contracted providers to perform above minimum standards.

Precision: The ability of an instrument to resolve small differences. Also known as *resolution*.

Predicted value: The statistically expected response or outcome for a patient after the risk adjustment model has been applied and the patient's unique set of risk factors have been taken into account.

Predictive modeling: The use of a software program to predict, with quantifiable accuracy, future indicator values, based on past data. This past data typically includes data not directly related to the data used to calculate the indicator.

Preferred provider organization (PPO): A form of managed care that has contracts with physicians, hospitals, and other providers of care who offer medical services to enrollees on a fee-for-service basis.

Prescriptive standard: A standard set as a goal that ought to be achieved or as a threshold that defines minimum performance. This standard may be derived from studies using different measurement methods.

Prevalence: The proportion of people in the entire population who have a disease at a certain point in time without regard to when they first got the disease.

Prevention: The degree to which appropriate services are provided for the promotion, preservation, and restoration of health and the early detection of disease.

Primary care department: A unit or clinic within the hospital that provides primary care services through hospital-salaried medical and/or nursing staff, focusing on evaluating and diagnosing medical problems and providing medical treatment on an outpatient basis.

Primary care network: A group of primary care physicians who contract among themselves and/or with health plans.

Process: An interrelated series of events, activities, actions, mechanisms, or steps that transform inputs into outputs.

Process management: An evaluation and restructuring of system functions to make sure certain processes are carried out in the most efficient and economical way.

Process map: A graphical description of a process, showing the sequence of process tasks, that is developed for a specific purpose and from a selected viewpoint.

Process measure: A measure that focuses on a process that leads to a certain outcome.

Process optimization: The removal or re-engineering of processes that don't add significant value to product or service, impede time to market, or result in suboptimal quality.

Profiling: The process of taking a few key customer data points, such as name, occupation, age, and address, and generating best guesses about their other characteristics.

Profit center: A segment of the healthcare enterprise for which costs, revenues, and profits are separately calculated.

Profit margin: Net profit after taxes divided by sales for a given 12-month period, expressed as a percentage.

Profit: The positive gain from business operations after subtracting all expenses.

Proprietary: Owned, copyrighted, or for which exclusive legal rights are held.

Prospective payment: Any advance payment to a provider or facility for future healthcare services. Capitation is a form of prospective payment.

Prospective Payment System (PPS): A reimbursement program in which Medicare pays a predetermined amount for each inpatient discharge.

Protected health information (PHI): Individually identifiable health information (HIPAA).

Protocol: A way of doing things that has become an agreed-upon convention. Alternatively, a set of standards that defines communications between computers.

Provider data: Provider-generated data not necessarily contained in the medical record.

Provider profile: An examination of services provided, claims filed, and benefits allocated by healthcare facilities, physicians, and other providers to assess quality of care and cost management.

Proxy for outcome: A process of care used as an indicator of health status, such as an admission to hospital used as an indication of increased severity of illness.

Psychologist/nonphysician behavioral health clinicians: Persons legally qualified by education and training to practice in the field of mental health.

Public domain: Belonging to the community at large, unprotected by copyright, and subject to appropriation by anyone.

Public health professionals: Persons educated in public health or a related discipline who are employed to improve health of populations.

Push technology: The automatic delivery of web news and other information without a request from the user.

Qualified providers: NCQA accreditation measure that verifies each physician in a health plan is licensed and trained to practice medicine and that the health plan's members are happy with their service.

Quality: A standard of service established by the healthcare enterprise, patients, or credentialing body.

Quality assurance: An assessment of the delivery portion of healthcare plans to make sure patients are receiving high-quality care when and where they need it.

Quality bonus: Monies for performance improvement.

Quality function deployment (QFD): Prioritizing and translating customer needs into technical requirements and then delivering a quality product or service that aims to satisfy the customer.

Quality management: The process of ensuring care is accessible and available, delivered within community standards, and that there is a system to identify and correct problems and to monitor ongoing performance.

Quality measure: A mechanism to assign a quantity to quality of care by comparison to a criterion.

Quality of care: Degree to which health services for individuals and populations increase the likelihood of desired health outcomes and are consistent with current professional knowledge.

Quality of life measure: A score based on a patient's overall well-being.

Quality Tools: A clearinghouse for quality assessment indicators sponsored by the Agency for Healthcare Research and Quality.

Random sample: A subset selected in such a way that each member of the population has an equal opportunity to be selected.

Randomization: A technique for selecting or assigning cases such that each case has an equal probability of being selected or assigned.

Range: The difference between the largest and smallest number in a set. A measure of the spread of a data set.

Rate: A score derived by dividing the number of cases that meet a criterion for quality by the number of eligible cases within a given time frame where the numerator cases are a subset of the denominator cases.

Rate of return: The annual return on an investment, expressed as a percentage of the total amount invested.

Rate based: An aggregate data measure in which the value of each measurement is expressed as a proportion or as a ratio.

Ratio: A relationship between two counted sets of data, which may have a value of zero or greater. In a ratio, the numerator is not necessarily a subset of the denominator.

Rationale: An explanation of why an indicator is useful in specifying and assessing the process or outcome of care measured by the indicator.

Real time: Computer communications or processes that are so fast they seem instantaneous.

Receiver operating characteristic (ROC): A graph obtained by plotting all sensitivity values on the y-axis against their equivalent values for all available thresholds on the x-axis.

Re-engineering: The process of analyzing, modeling, and streamlining internal processes so that a company can deliver better-quality products and services.

Referred visit: A visits to a specialty unit of the hospital established for providing technical aid used in the diagnosis and treatment of patients.

Refined Diagnostic-Related Group (RDRG): A version of the DRG program that classifies cases into levels of severity and complexity based on the impact they are likely to have on use of hospital resources.

Registry data: Those data obtained from local, regional, or national disease or procedure-related registries.

Regression: A mathematical method of forecasting using line equations to explain the relationship between multiple causes and effects.

Regression coefficient: For a linear relationship, the constant that represents the rate of change of one variable as a function of changes in the other.

Rehabilitation centers: Facilities that provide programs for rehabilitating individuals with mental illnesses, drug or alcohol addictions, or physical disabilities.

Rehabilitation service: An organization service providing medical, health-related, social, and vocational services for disabled persons to help them attain or retain their maximum functional capacity.

Reimbursement: Payment for medical services delivered.

Relational database: A database where all information is arranged in tables containing predefined fields.

Relative value unit (RVU): A composite measure of the time, difficulty, and resources associated with a procedure or service, used to establish fees, reimbursement levels, and physician incentives.

Relevance: The applicability and/or pertinence of the indicator to its users and customers.

Reliability: The degree to which the measure is free from random error.

Reliability, availability, serviceability (RAS): An evaluation method weighs a system's performance and maintenance/repair record to determine whether or not the productivity of the system is worth the cost to maintain it.

Remittance advice: A notice of payment due, either in paper form or as a notice of an electronic data interchange financial transaction.

Repeatability: The ability of an instrument or system to provide consistent results.

Reporting period: The defined time period that describes the patient's end of service.

Request for proposal (RFP): A document that requests prospective service providers to propose the term, conditions, and other elements of an agreement to deliver specified services.

Requirements specification: A description, in operational terms, of what management expects the vendor's product or service to do for the company.

Residential care facilities: Long-term care facilities that provide supervision and assistance in the activities of daily living with medical and nursing services when required.

Residual value: The value remaining in a device as a function of time. The longer the time from the original purchase date, the lower the residual value.

Retained earnings: The portion of an organization's net earnings not paid to shareholders in the form of dividends.

Retention: The result when members remain on a health plan from one year to the next. Alternatively, the percentage of a premium that a health plan keeps for internal costs or profit.

Return on assets (ROA): The ratio of operating earnings to net operating assets. The ROA is a test of whether a business is earning enough to cover its cost of capital

Return on equity (ROE): The ratio of net income to the owner's equity. The ROE is a measure of the return on investment for an owner's equity capital invested in the organization.

Return on investment (ROI): Profit resulting from investing in a process or piece of equipment. The profit could be money, time savings, or other positive results.

Revenue: The inflow of assets from providing services to patients.

Risk-adjusted measures: Those measures that are risk adjusted using statistical modeling or stratification methods.

Risk-adjusted rate: A rate that takes into account differences in case mix to enable valid comparisons between groups.

Risk adjustment: A statistical process for reducing, removing, or clarifying the influences of confounding factors that differ among comparison groups.

Risk adjustment data elements: Those data elements used to risk adjust a performance measure.

Risk adjustment model: The statistical algorithm that specifies the numerical values and the sequence of calculations used to risk adjust performance measures.

Risk factor: A variable describing some characteristic of individual patients that may influence healthcare-related outcomes.

Risk factor value: A specific value assigned to a risk factor for a given episode of care (EOC) record.

Risk model: The statistical algorithm that specifies the numerical values and the sequence of calculations used to risk adjust performance measures.

Risk sharing: An arrangement that combines the risk of financial losses for all care providers in a business entity such as a hospital or physician group. One provider's losses are shared by all, but gains also are shared.

Rollout: The process of introducing a new technology-based service.

Root cause analysis: A step-by-step approach that leads to the identification of a fault's first or root cause.

Rural healthcare: Healthcare services, public or private, in rural areas.

Rural populations: Persons inhabiting rural areas or small towns classified as rural.

Safety: The degree to which the risk of an intervention and the risk in the care environment are reduced for the patient and others, including the healthcare provider.

Sales: Total dollar amount collected for services provided.

Salvage value: The estimated price for which a fixed asset can be sold at the end of its useful life.

Sample: A subset of the population selected according to some scheme.

Sample size: The number of individuals or particular patients included in a study.

Sampling design: The procedure for selecting a subset of a population to observe or estimate a characteristic of the entire population.

Sampling method: The process used to select a sample. Possible approaches to sampling include simple random sampling, cluster sampling, systematic sampling, and judgment sampling.

Sampling: The process of selecting a group of units, portions of material, or observations from a larger collection of units, quantity of material, or observations that serves to provide information that may be used as a basis for making a decision concerning the larger quantity.

Satisfaction measures: Indicators that assess the extent to which the patients/enrollees, practitioners, and/or purchasers perceive their needs to be met.

Satisfaction survey: A survey sent to members of a health plan to allow feedback on the organization's service and quality.

Scheduled survey date: The date an organization is to begin its full survey.

Score: A rating, usually expressed as a number, and based on the degree to which certain qualities or attributes are present.

Scorecard: A table of the key performance indicators tracked by an organization. A Balanced Scorecard is a particular type of scorecard.

Self-insured: A company that creates and maintains its own health plan for its employees instead of contracting with an outside insurance provider. Also called *self-funded*.

Sensitivity: In statistics, the percentage of actual positives that are counted as positive.

Sentient computing: A computing system in which computers, telephones, and everyday objects track the identities and locations of users and predicts their needs.

Sentinel event: Relatively infrequent, clear-cut events that occur independently of a patient's condition that commonly reflect hospital system and process deficiencies and result in unnecessary outcomes for patients.

Server: A computer that controls access to the network and net-based resources.

Service-level agreement (SLA): An agreement between the parent corporation or other customer and the shared services unit in which the unit agrees to provide services to a specified performance level.

Service mix index (SMI): The average relative weight of the procedures billed for a service.

Severity: The degree of biomedical risk, morbidity, or mortality of medical treatment.

Shared risk payment: A payment arrangement in which a hospital and a managed care organization share the risk of adverse claims experience.

Shareholders' equity: What the owners of the organization have left when all liabilities have been met. The difference between total assets and total liabilities.

Sigma: In statistics, the unit of standard deviation.

Simple random sample: A process in which a predetermined number of cases from a population as a whole is selected for review.

Single-photon emission computed tomography (SECT): A nuclear medicine imaging technology that combines the existing technology of gamma camera imaging with computed tomographic imaging technology to provide a more precise and clear image.

Six Sigma: A statistically driven quality management methodology designed to reduce defects and variations in a business process, thereby increasing customer satisfaction and business profits. The stated goal is to reduce defects to a level equal to six standard deviations (sigma) from the mean.

Slack: In the context of project management, the time in which a minor process or activity can be completed in advance of the next major operation or activity that depends on it.

Social capital: The sum of the resources embedded within, available through, and derived from the network of relationships possessed by an individual or social unit.

Social workers: Individuals trained and certified in the field of social work.

Sourcing: The process of identifying potential suppliers of specified services or goods.

Special cause variation: Variation due to specific factors and not due to random error.

Special or unique data source: A data source that is unique to an organization and inaccessible to outside entities or persons.

Specificity: The percentage of actual negatives that are rejected.

Stability: The ability of an instrument or device to provide repeatable results over time.

Staff model HMO: An HMO variation where the staff physicians work only for a single HMO and have no private practices.

Staffing ratios: Clinical hospital staff to patient ratios.

Standard: A process, format, or transmission protocol that has become convention by the agreement of a group of users.

Standard deviation: A measure of dispersion in the sample, calculated by taking the square root of the variance.

Standard industry code (SIC): Codes assigned to various industries and jobs.

Standard of quality: A generally accepted, objective standard of measurement against which an individual's or organization's level of performance may be compared.

Standards: Agreed principles of protocol set by government, trade, and international organizations that govern behavior.

Statement of retained earnings: A report on how much of the organization's earnings were not paid out in dividends.

Statistic: A number resulting from the manipulation of sample data according to specific procedures.

Statistical process control (SPC): A method of differentiating between acceptable variations from variations that could indicate problems, based on statistical probability.

Strategic management system: The use of the balanced scorecard in aligning an organization's short-term actions with strategy.

Strategic resource allocation: The process of aligning budgets with strategy by using the balanced scorecard to make resource allocation decisions.

Strategic services: Processes that directly affect an enterprise's ability to compete.

Strategy map: The interrelationships among measures that weave together to describe an organization's strategy.

Strategy: The differentiating activities an organization pursues to gain competitive advantage.

Stratification: A form of risk adjustment that involves classifying data into subgroups based on one or more characteristics, variables, or other categories.

Stratified measure: A performance measure that is classified into a number of subgroups to assist in analysis and interpretation.

Structure chart: A graphic description of a process that shows the modular structure of a system, the hierarchy into which the modules are arranged, and the data and control interfaces among modules.

Structure measure: A measure that assesses whether organizational resources and arrangements are in place to deliver healthcare, such as the number, type, and distribution of medical personnel, equipment, and facilities.

Structured Query Language (SQL): A standard command language used to interact with databases.

Subacute care: Medical and skilled nursing services provided to patients who are not in an acute phase of illness but who require a level of care higher than that provided in a long-term care setting.

Subrogation: An agreement by which the primary insurer can collect funds from a patient's other benefits sources as reimbursement for claim costs.

Subsidiary: A company that is wholly controlled by another or one that is more than 50% owned by another organization.

Subsidiary medical record (SMR): A medical record maintained by a specific department.

Sunk cost: Investments made in the past that have no bearing on future investment decisions.

Supply chain management: Managing the movement of goods from raw materials to the finished product delivered to customers.

Supply chain: The flow of materials, information, and finances as they move in a process from supplier to manufacturer to wholesaler to retailer to consumer.

Swing bed: Temporary nursing home care in a hospital setting. Hospitals offering swing beds have fewer than 100 beds, are located in a rural region, and provide 24-hour nursing care.

Synergy: The benefit derived from the cooperation between two business entities.

Systematic random sampling: A process in which one case is selected randomly and the next cases are selected according to a fixed period or interval.

Systematized Nomenclature of Human and Veterinary Medicine (SNOMED): A standardized vocabulary system for medical databases.

Systems integration: The merging of diverse hardware, software, and communications systems into a consolidated operating unit.

Tangible asset: Assets having a physical existence, such as cash, equipment, and real estate, as well as accounts receivable.

Target: The desired result of a performance measure. Targets make meaningful the results derived from measurement and provide organizations with feedback regarding performance.

Taxonomy: The classification of concepts and objects into a hierarchically ordered system that indicates relationships.

Telemedicine: A segment of telehealth that focuses on the provider aspects of healthcare telecommunications, especially medical imaging technology.

Telemonitoring: Monitoring patient physiologic parameters, images, or other data from a distance.

Tertiary care: Care that requires highly specialized skills, technology, and support services.

Test cases: Fictitious patient-level data composed of clinical data elements that yield an expected result for a specific core measure algorithm.

Third-party administrator: A company independent of a healthcare organization that handles claims and/or other business services.

Third-party payer: An insurance company, health maintenance organization, or government agency that pays for medical services for a patient.

Tiering: A cost-sharing model used by purchasers and health plans to encourage the selection of better performing, more effective and efficient providers.

Timeliness: The degree to which care is provided to the patient at the most beneficial or necessary time.

Total cost of ownership (TCO): The cost of owning a device or technology, including operating expenses.

Total expenses: All payroll and nonpayroll expenses as well as any nonoperating losses.

Total quality management (TQM): A customer-centric philosophy based on constant improvement to meet customer demands.

Touch point: The point of contact between a patient and a healthcare enterprise.

Transients/migrants: Mobile, short-term residents who move, usually to find work.

Transmission schedule: The schedule of dates on which performance measurement systems are expected to be transmitting data.

Trend analysis: The percentage change in indicator value from a reference or base year—that is, [(subsequent − base year)/base year] × 100.

Trended: The application of trend analysis on a performance indicator.

Triage: A means of guiding patients to proper services by using an intermediary person to gather preliminary information and answer patients' questions.

Uniform billing code: The procedural rules on patient billing, including what information should appear on the bill and how it should be coded.

Urgent care center: A facility that provides care and treatment for problems that are not life threatening but require attention over the short term.

Useful life: The time, usually expressed in months or years, that a device can perform a useful function.

User interface: The junction between the user and the computer.

Usual and customary: An insurance industry term for a charge that is usual and customary and made by persons having similar medical conditions in the county of the policyholder.

Utilization management: A review process used to make sure a patient's hospital stay, surgery, tests, or other treatment is necessary.

Validity: The degree to which the measure is associated with what it purports to measure.

Value chain: The sequence of events in the process of delivering healthcare.

Value proposition: A description of how an organization will differentiate itself to customers, and what particular set of values it will deliver.

Value-added network (VAN): An information exchange network between a healthcare site and its business operations such as billing and supply offices.

Values: The deeply held beliefs within the enterprise that are demonstrated through the day-to-day behaviors of all employees.

Variable: A phenomenon that may take on different values.

Variable cost: A unit cost that depends on total volume.

Variance: A measure of dispersion in a sample, calculated by taking the average of square differences between observations and their mean.

Virtual knowledge management: A knowledge management model in which knowledge workers and management work and communicate through the web and other networks.

Vision: A shared mental framework that helps give form to the often-abstract future that lies ahead.

Wage index: A measure of the relative differences in the average hourly wage for the hospitals in each labor market area compared to the national average hourly wage.

Warranty: A contractual undertaking given by the supplier to provide a specified level of product or service support.

Web service: A tool or capability that can be accessed through the web, rather than being run locally on a desktop.

Weighted index: An index adjusted to reflect the differential importance of variables relative to other values.

Weighted mean: The sum of the mean of each group multiplied by its respective weights, divided by the sum of the weights.

Weighted score: A combination of the values of several items into a single summary value for each case where each item is differentially weighted.

Workflow: A process description of how tasks are done, by whom, in what order, and how quickly.

Working capital: The funds available for current operating needs. Computationally, it is current assets less current liabilities.

Zero defects: A management strategy practice that aims to reduce defects in products or services as a way to increase profits.

Index